Grey Gardens

Matthew Tinkcom

palgrave
macmillan

A BFI book published by Palgrave Macmillan

In Memory of Michael Ragussis

**791.
437
2
GRE**

First published in 2011 by
PALGRAVE MACMILLAN

on behalf of the

BRITISH FILM INSTITUTE
21 Stephen Street, London W1T 1LN
www.bfi.org.uk

There's more to discover about film and television through the BFI. Our world-renowned archive,
cinemas, festivals, films, publications and learning resources are here to inspire you.

Palgrave Macmillan in the UK is an imprint of Macmillan Publishers Limited, registered in
England, company number 785998, of Houndmills, Basingstoke, Hampshire RG21 6XS. Palgrave
Macmillan in the US is a division of St Martin's Press LLC, 175 Fifth Avenue, New York, NY 10010.
Palgrave Macmillan is the global academic imprint of the above companies and has companies
and representatives throughout the world. Palgrave® and Macmillan® are registered trademarks
in the United States, the United Kingdom, Europe and other countries.

Series cover design: Ashley Western
Series text design: ketchup/SE14
Images from *Grey Gardens*, © Portrait Films, Inc.

Set by Cambrian Typesetters, Camberley, Surrey
Printed in China

This book is printed on paper suitable for recycling and made from fully managed and sustained
forest sources. Logging, pulping and manufacturing processes are expected to conform to the
environmental regulations of the country of origin.

British Library Cataloguing-in-Publication Data
A catalogue record for this book is available from the British Library
A catalog record for this book is available from the Library of Congress
10 9 8 7 6 5 4 3 2 1
20 19 18 17 16 15 14 13 12 11

ISBN 978-1-84457-395-0

BFI Film (

405222

The BFI Film Classics is a series of books that introduces, interprets and celebrates landmarks of world cinema. Each volume offers an argument for the film's 'classic' status, together with discussion of its production and reception history, its place within a genre or national cinema, an account of its technical and aesthetic importance, and in many cases, the author's personal response to the film.

For a full list of titles available in the series, please visit our website: <www.palgrave.com/bfi>

'Magnificently concentrated examples of flowing freeform critical poetry.'
Uncut

'A formidable body of work collectively generating some fascinating insights into the evolution of cinema.'
Times Higher Education Supplement

'The series is a landmark in film criticism.'
Quarterly Review of Film and Video

Contents

Introduction

I made Grey Gardens in order to get some food for my mother.

Little Edie Beale

In early February of 1954, Edith Ewing Bouvier Beale sent a telegram from Easthampton, New York, to her brother, John Vernou Bouvier III, in New York City. It read:

STILL WAITING FOR MY MONTHLY CHECK. SEND IMMEDIATELY. URGENT. TERRIBLY COLD AND DANGEROUS HERE FOR ME; MUST ARRANGE TO COME TO CITY … PLEASE ACT IMMEDIATELY; THIS IS MY SEVENTH WINTER HERE. PLEASE UNDERSTAND. EDITH.

John Bouvier or 'Black Jack', as Mrs Beale's brother was known within the family, was the father of future US first lady Jacqueline Bouvier Kennedy Onassis and was the trustee for Edith Beale's inheritance from the Wall Street law firm of Bouvier and Beale. Edith Beale – or 'Big Edie', as she came to be known – had, since her separation from her husband in the early 1930s, relied upon the proceeds of the Bouvier family trust to maintain her household in Easthampton. The urgency of her message – particularly the fact that it was by then her seventh year living in the family's summer house at Grey Gardens – was probably borne of the fact that she was supporting not only herself but also her unmarried daughter. Her (only) daughter, also named Edith and nicknamed 'Little Edie', had lived with her since 1952 after a modelling career in New York had, under circumstances that are still unclear, come to an end, at which point she had returned to live with her mother on Long Island.

Although it remains unknown whether Edith Ewing Beale received any immediate aid from her brother in response to her telegram, what is known is that the situation would not improve for nearly another twenty years. In 1972, the modest financial circumstances to which the two women had become accustomed became known to the Suffolk County Health Department and, in an event that would receive widespread newspaper and television coverage, their home was deemed uninhabitable; only after their relative, Jacqueline Bouvier Kennedy Onassis, intervened and underwrote the cleaning and partial renovation of the house, were they allowed to remain there. Although the help that Onassis provided allowed the women to stay in the house for several more years, it hardly altered their circumstances beyond the genteel – and extreme – poverty that they had come to know.

The financial conditions that led the Beales to the situation in which they found themselves living for nearly four decades would probably be of little interest to anyone beyond devotees of the life of Jacqueline Kennedy Onassis were it not for the fact that they became the subjects of a film that has come to inhabit a special place in the visual culture of the United States in the 1970s and in the history of the documentary film, Albert and David Maysles' *Grey Gardens*. Filmed over the course of six weeks late in the summer of 1973 and released in 1975, the film has achieved a cult status among its audience; further, it has been the sponsoring text for a number of productions, including a subsequent documentary release by Albert Maysles (*The Beales of Grey Gardens*, 2006), an off-Broadway play, a Broadway musical, a 2009 feature fiction film made for the HBO cable channel that featured actresses Jessica Lange and Drew Barrymore, a documentary about the making of the original film, Liliana Greenfield-Sanders' *Ghosts of Grey Gardens*, as well as any number of drag performances, fashion designs by such figures as John Bartlett, Marc Jacobs and Todd Oldham, websites, blogs, fan publications and art. Clearly, the danger that Big Edie telegraphed to her brother so long ago has taken hold within the imaginations of the many audiences for *Grey Gardens*.

What, though, is the appeal of this film? Why does this ninety-five-minute cinematic portrait of a mother and daughter talking, eating, listening to music, discussing family photographs, feeding their many pets and bickering over events that had occurred decades previously fascinate its viewers? Even within the Maysles brothers' substantial oeuvre of documentary, or, as they preferred to call it, 'direct cinema', which includes such canonical titles as *What's Happening! The Beatles in America* (1964), *Salesman* (1968) and *Gimme Shelter* (1970), *Grey Gardens* has come to have a unique status as a film that altered the possibilities of the documentary image. It did so by allowing the non-fiction film to organize its materials through two previously unexamined aspects of everyday life: first, the psychodynamics of the family – in particular, the bond between mother and daughter – and, second, the role of fantasy in femininity and glamour, not least in fashion culture. Further, it introduced a particular relation between film-maker and photographic subject that can only be called a seduction, whereby the person being photographed – in this case, Little Edie Beale – woos and courts David Maysles, the brother responsible for the film's soundtrack. While other projects in the moving-image culture of the period had also inaugurated the documentary into similar concerns, not least the films of Andy Warhol in the 1960s, the performance films of Shirley Clarke, such as *The Connection* (1962) and *Portrait of Jason* (1967), and the US public television series, *An American Family* (which aired in the year of *Grey Gardens*' production), the images and sounds of Big Edie and Little Edie brought these three fascinations together in a way that remains still pertinent to the film's audience after over thirty years.

Indeed, it is remarkable that *Grey Gardens* has endured and its fascinations have become even more pronounced since its original release, particularly in the past decade. This in part can be explained as a result of new distribution modes for the film – the VHS tape, DVD, cable and satellite channels, web-facilitated commentary – all make the film available to new audiences. This fact, though, fails to address the appeal of the film's narrative and protagonists, and worth noting is that the Maysleses crafted *Grey Gardens* with immense care

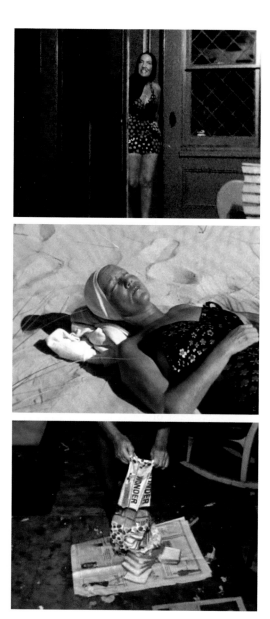

and deliberation; after primary photography ended in the autumn of 1973, it took nearly two years to edit the seventy-two hours of raw footage into a film that runs for just over an hour and a half. Working with three editors – Ellen Hovde, Muffie Meyer and Susan Froemke – the Maysleses distilled the 16mm footage into a seemingly simple story about the bond between Big Edie and Little Edie. Yet, despite the fact that it may seem at times to have a meandering and casual pacing, the film in fact derives its affective pull on the viewer by having a carefully orchestrated narrative that builds up to an emotionally fraught conversation between mother and daughter about the latter's sense of imprisonment in the household and the blame she assigns to Big Edie for her never having married.

In order for this concluding conversation to have its impact, the film maintains a structure in which we alternately witness the two women in conversation and then subsequently gain access to Little Edie's own thoughts about her predicament. At very few moments in the film are we privy to Big Edie's feelings in the same manner as the private conversations between the film-makers and Little Edie – such as when she greets them at the door, gives them a tour of the garden, sun-bathes on the beach and feeds raccoons in the house's attic. In this light, it is hardly surprising that Little Edie has emerged over the past thirty-five years as the figure around whom the film revolves. This helps to make sense of the film's iconic poster: a photograph shows Little Edie as she sports a deteriorating fur coat while her head is wrapped in a scarf and displays her signature brooch. She stands with her hand on her hip in front of the weather-beaten house in a winterish field of brown, and her facial expression locks the camera's gaze and poses the question that brings viewers back to Grey Gardens and to *Grey Gardens*: what am I doing here?

In order to answer this question, we can consider the film's story to be, in its most elemental terms, a series of conversations that Big Edie and Little Edie have about how they came to live the lives that they did. They do not address this question as directly as we might always like, and the film showcases the frequently oblique

terms by which they approach awkward topics, such as the mother's divorce, the daughter's ill health, past friends and lovers, and decline, grief and loss. Indeed, it often seems the case that the film holds its viewers' attention because these two women are so artful in their conversational indirection, and, even when they seem to be blunt in their assertions, it frequently seems the case that they are only partly expressing what they think about a given subject. Here, the film takes advantage of its status *as film*, as visual and acoustic record, because their facial expressions, postures, tones of voice and gestures reveal (and conceal) as much as the explicit things they say in conversation.

Because of this continual deflection, substitution and allusion within their talk, the film invites and, in fact, seems to demand that the viewer be alert to the interpretive work brought about by all this refusal by the Beales ever to be direct and specific in their conversation, and part of the pleasure of the film is the attempt to make sense of what exactly the two women are getting at. For example, in a typical exchange that still baffles this writer, Little Edie tells the film-makers that her mother 'doesn't like the Catholic Church', to which we hear her mother (who has overheard the comment) shoot back, 'Oh, go on, what the hell, I worship the Catholic Church!' While it is tempting to consider how the context of this banter would help to explain what exactly this all means, it also becomes apparent in the film that the Beales are endlessly revisiting (and revising) their memories of the past, and in this case 'the Catholic Church' could mean any number of things, from marriage to thoughts about the metaphysical to their relations to specific family members, priests and friends.

The thrust of all this interpretive work, which the film invites from its viewers, is that it heralded, in its making and in its subsequent lives with audiences, the reinvention of documentary cinema from an activity of scientific and ostensibly objective recording of natural and human phenomena to a new and dynamic set of relations among the film's subjects, the film-makers and its audiences, all of whom come to have a stake in making sense of what exactly it is that the Beales are getting at. In this regard, *Grey Gardens* marks a new role for non-fiction film, one more like a literary text such as the novel and less like the heavy-handed instructional film which it had previously been. Historians and critics of documentary cinema have noticed this shift in the historical moment in which *Grey Gardens* was made – the early 1970s – but seldom have attended to the specific aspects of this film that have made it such an enduring fascination for its viewers.

In order to understand the change in the non-fiction film in which *Grey Gardens* marks a signal moment, it is important to consider that the 'direct cinema' movement in which Albert and David Maysles were central figures sought to do multiple things that might often seem to be at odds with one another: to be, on the one hand, what Bill Nichols has called the 'observational' documentary, whereby the film-maker seeks as much as possible to remain outside the frame and to let the events depicted unfold with seemingly little guidance by the film-maker – what is sometimes referred to as the 'fly-on-wall' aesthetic of the direct cinema movement – while functioning, on the other, whether the film-maker intends it or not, as what Nichols calls an 'interactive' mode of non-fiction cinema, where the relation between the subject and the documentarian is part of what is being articulated for the viewer.[1]

In this regard, the direct cinema movement emerged, in the 1960s, as a loosely affiliated group of younger documentary film-makers who sought to take advantage of technological changes that allowed for cameras and sound equipment to become lighter and therefore more mobile – the film-maker could more nimbly move to where the action was and thus new subjects for documentary could be more 'directly' recorded. As Paul Ward describes it, 'the developments in portable cameras and sound recording equipment, in the late 1950s, led to a documentary practice that was much more able to exploit the immediacy and "behind-the-scenes" feel of social events and situations'.[2] Thus, the camera's new mobility encouraged a sense that it bore witness to events that might occur in the absence of documentation anyway, while, in fact, although the camera was lightweight and sat upon the shoulder of a film-maker, the film-maker was also, regardless of his wishes to seem invisible, a participant and sponsor to the event.

Perhaps the abiding fascination of direct cinema films and their makers is that they can be understood as attempting to inhabit this seeming contradiction: both to be in the film and not to be in it – the film-makers associated with the direct cinema of the 1960s frequently attempted both these things. One way of making sense of how the film-maker might reside within his film – and the group was composed almost entirely of men, with the exception of the editors (more on that below) – is to see the topics of direct cinema films as the place where the film-makers introduce us to their way of looking at the world. With this in mind, we can see the particular notion of the social and political worlds that direct cinema film-makers sought to record as the domain of men and masculinity, as public and as institutional. The canonical documentary films of the decade prior to *Grey Gardens*' release – films by D. A. Pennebaker, Richard Leacock, Frederick Wiseman and the Maysleses – are almost entirely concerned with masculinity, its institutions and its performances: popular music (*Don't Look Back*, *Monterey Pop*, *What's Happening!*, *Gimme Shelter*), the public spheres of politics (*Primary*), education and health (*Titicut Follies*, *High School*, *Law and Order*, *Hospital*).

Michael Renov tells us that the practitioners of direct cinema, 'tended … to be under the influence of the natural sciences in their early pronouncements of an ethic of nonintervention, even artistic selflessness' and that 'the observational mode … of documentary film-making [that was] often called direct cinema, [was] characterized by the prevalence of indirect address, the use of long takes and synchronous sound, tending toward spatiotemporal continuity rather than montage, evoking a feeling of the "present tense" '.[3] According to Renov, direct cinema assumed a unique status for the non-fiction film-maker who could think of himself as removed from the action that unfolds before him and yet is implicated in its production. Ultimately, the project of direct cinema seems to have derived its greatest fascination when this paradox about it seems most pronounced: the film-maker could not assume that his presence was irrelevant as a motivation for the action that unfolded before his camera because he participated in the film's events. What sponsored the change – whereby direct cinema's 'scientific' impulse was revealed to be the observer's paradox (i.e., witnessing an event shapes that event) – was the emergence of new subjects for the camera: women, gays, blacks, the socially exiled – who no longer would remain objects of scrutiny simply to be recorded like so many objects in the documentary cinema's museum. In this regard, the paradox might have remained tenable were it not, according to Renov, for the fact that direct cinema occurred at the same time as important changes in identity politics, such as feminism, the black power movements of the 1960s and post-Stonewall gay and lesbian politics. That is, there was simultaneous discovery that the white male 'universal' observer/film-maker was not exempt from having an identity politics; Renov comments that 'these white male professionals had assumed the mantle of filmic representation with the ease and self-assurance of a birthright', while the newly unfolding worlds of women, racial minorities and gay/lesbian people began to discover that 'the self-enactments are transgressive. Through their explorations of the (social) self, they are speaking the lives and desires of the many who have lived outside "the boundaries of cultural knowledge".'[4]

The critical response to direct cinema's products was not always positive regarding the style's outcomes. In one of the most famous attacks on the project, Pauline Kael wrote about the Maysleses' film *Gimme Shelter* that the film-makers were guilty of 'questionable ethics' in which they exploited the events that they claimed to have dispassionately recorded – in this instance, the murder of an audience member at a Rolling Stones' concert, which the camera recorded and which is included in the final moments of *Gimme Shelter*. Kael recognised the difficulty in assigning blame to the film-makers, writing that:

with modern documentarians, as with many TV news cameramen, it's impossible to draw a clear line between catching actual events and arranging events to be caught ... there are no simple ethical standards to apply, and, because the situations are so fluid and variable, one has to be fairly knowledgeable not to get suckered into reacting to motion-picture footage that appears to be documentary as if it were the simple truth.[5]

Having said that, she then excoriates the Maysleses for exploiting the Rolling Stones' fame and for being disingenuous in claiming that they could document such an event without understanding that they were playing into the hands of the band, its promoters and the concert's financial underwriters. While not blaming the film-makers specifically for the violence and death that their cameras captured on film, Kael claims that 'big stars cooperate only if they get financial – and generally, artistic – control of the film', and that the Maysleses' least dishonourable claim might be that they could not have understood how the presence of their cameras could have incited behaviours that otherwise might not have occurred. Further, Kael finishes her commentary by telling us that 'it's impossible to say how much movie-making itself is responsible for those consequences, but it is a factor, and with the commercial success of this kind of film it's going to be a bigger factor'. In sum, Kael suggested that she considered the Maysleses to be guilty of a faux naïveté about the effects their film-making had on audiences – both those within a film like *Gimme Shelter* and those for the film in its theatrical screenings.

The Maysleses responded to Kael's damning review with a letter in which they defended themselves by arguing that the film was indeed about the very problem she articulates – the effects of fame on the famous and on their fans – and did not seek to exploit such notoriety but to ask questions about it. They comment about Kael's review that:

all the evidence she uses in her analysis of their [i.e., the Rolling Stones] disturbing relationship to their audience is evidence supplied by the film, by the structure of the film which tries to render in its maximum complexity the very problems of [Mick] Jagger's double self, of his insolent appeal and the fury it can and in fact does provoke, and even the pathos of his final powerlessness.

The film-makers sought to exonerate themselves from Kael's accusations by suggesting that no one emerges in heroic fashion from the film and that 'rather than giving the audience what it wants to believe the film forces the audiences to see things as they are'.

It is worth dwelling upon this exchange between the critic and the film-makers in order to understand how *Grey Gardens*, the next film that the Maysleses produced after *Gimme Shelter*, can be read as a response to the accusation that they sought to exploit their subjects. Here, the subjects (i.e., the Edies) were eager for exposure, and indeed the history of *Grey Gardens*' production is instructive. According to Albert Maysles, Lee Radziwell (the sister of Jacqueline Bouvier Kennedy Onassis) contacted him and his brother in the early 1970s with an idea to make a film about various people whom Radziwell had known in the Hamptons, the wealthy Atlantic-coast resort where New York City's privileged have been building summer houses since the late nineteenth century. Among the figures whom the Maysleses recorded in that initial project – one underwritten by Radziwell herself – were her aunt and cousin (i.e., Big Edie and Little Edie). After an initial ninety-minute cut of that footage was screened for her, an appalled Radziwell insisted on taking possession of the negative, which she did. (According to Hovde, the squalor in the house at that point was even more pronounced than that which ultimately appears in *Grey Gardens* because principle photography took place before the mansion had been cleaned up for the health authorities; as Hovde comments, the film had 'more racoons' than in the *Grey Gardens* that we know.) According to Albert Maysles, a year later he and his brother re-contacted the Beales about a possible new project in which they would be the central subjects, and they were eager to participate. At that point the project that would become *Grey Gardens* began to take shape.

However, the sense that the Beales were vulnerable – financially and emotionally – to the Maysleses' attentions and thus liable to be taken advantage of has haunted many viewers of the film, and in this regard *Grey Gardens* serves as one of the first instances in the redefinition of documentary film and video that leads to the present moment, where participants in such media productions as *Big Brother*, *Survivor* and their like participate in the disclosure of intimacies and personal knowledge – much of it deliberately distasteful and capable of producing discomfort in its audiences. This is not to dispel entirely the abiding problem of the relation between documentarian and subject, which predates the work of the Maysleses to the earliest moments of non-fiction cinema – but to recognise the central role that *Grey Gardens* plays in a genealogy of the documentary image after the direct cinema movement. That is, this film is key to understanding how the domain of the private and domestic lives of documentary subjects became fair game for the non-fiction camera in ways that it had not previously been.

It is important to historicise the film as part of the new emphasis on sexual and gender politics which had begun in the 1960s and, by the moment of the film's appearance, had become a central part of political discourse in North America and in the UK. This politics more frequently goes by the name of 'feminism'. While it is not the case that the Maysleses ever identify themselves with this movement, we are well served to recall that the film was ultimately edited into its final version not by the Maysleses but by Ellen Hovde, Muffie Meyer and Susan Froemke, and that Hovde and Meyer, alongside Albert and David Maysles, receive directorial credit for the film.

This emphasis on the collaborative dimensions of one of their film's production was not new for the Maysleses when *Grey Gardens* was produced. Starting with *Salesman* (1968), the Maysleses have consistently given directorial credits to the editors with whom they work to produce the final versions of their films, and in this regard we relearn the longstanding lesson of cinema: how key editing is to the look and shape of a film. It is no coincidence, then, that a film edited by three women in the mid-1970s, just as feminist political and intellectual projects became a part of daily life in the USA, so centrally concerns itself with the lives of two specific women and their relations to men, power, affluence and the choices they might make about how to live their lives. As Hovde comments on the DVD of the film, she, Meyer and Froemke spent two years working to shape the raw footage – seventy-two hours of film and an additional thirty hours of acoustic recordings – into the final ninety-five-minute product. This resulted in their having, according to Hovde, daily conversations about feminism as much as about the film and she suggests that it emerged as a feminist project about how the social class out of which the Bealeses emerged – affluent, conservative and focused on women as wives and mothers – informed the ways that they could live out their aspirations to be artists.

In light of this, *Grey Gardens* is perhaps best understood as a film in which Albert and David Maysles participated in the production of the images and sounds but which Hovde, Meyer and Froemke subsequently reshaped into a piece of direct cinema informed by many of the concerns of feminism at that historical juncture. This is not to say that the intent or outcome of *Grey Gardens* was feminist, but it could not help but be informed by the political and intellectual concerns of its moment and, more to the point, it ultimately resonated with its audiences because its depictions of talented, articulate and witty women becomes all the more poignant in light of the limited possibilities they encountered in the earlier periods of their lives. When, therefore, Little Edie announces at one point in the film that she is a 'staunch character: S-T-A-U-N-C-H', posing with her head wrapped in a towel and adorned with her mother's gold brooch, she probably had no sense that she was offering an icon of defiant femininity, but that indeed is what she has become.

At the same time that Little Edie's resoluteness as a 'staunch character' allows for her to become a feminist icon, she simultaneously begs the question of why she is so deeply enmeshed in

a relationship with her mother that seems often not to have moved beyond an infantile dependency. Put another way: if Little Edie is so tough, why at the age of fifty-six is she still living at home? Ellen Hovde suggests that this is the central question of the film when she remarks that the film ultimately is about the dependent relations – the bonds that cannot, for good or ill, be broken – and that Little Edie's reliance on her mother seems to have come about from, as Hovde euphemistically suggests, 'a break' that resulted in her returning home to be nursed by Big Edie.

What if the 'break' is that she simply refused, consciously or not, to marry in the conventional terms on offer and that the results, as they emerge in the film, were the consequences of poverty and alienation – but also of eccentric pleasure and self-invention? Little Edie evidently understands the consequences of how she has decided to live her life and such decisions have been shaped around the two very different figures of her mother and father. Edith Vernier Bouvier Beale was a talented amateur singer who lived the first part of her life in typical fashion among the wealthy and privileged elite of New York and New England. Phelan Beale, on the other hand, was a conservative and austere figure who seems to have frowned upon his wife and his daughter's aspirations to sing and to dance. If Little Edie undertook any guidance from them, she could see, in the case of her mother, that small deviations from social expectation carried grave consequences, while from her father she might understand how boring and uninspired convention might be – see, for example, her reading of his inscription to Big Edie on his portrait (discussed below).

While we can understand *Grey Gardens*, then, through the historical context in which feminist critics, activists and artists were questioning the social roles that women play – and, often, are prohibited from playing – in the larger public sphere, the space of the private household was also beginning to receive attention, only through another name: that of melodrama. And, as we shall see in the next chapter, Edith Vernier Bouvier Beale and Edith Bouvier Beale were, if nothing else, highly melodramatic.

1 'We Belong Together': Melodrama as Non-Fiction in *Grey Gardens*

There are some nice people in the world. I just don't happen to be related to any of them.

Little Edie Beale

At the heart of Little Edie's claim resides the recognition that it often seems that the family is where we witness the worst behaviours: jealousy, cruelty, indifference, hostility, the list goes one. Remarkable about Little Edie's revelation is that she would articulate such a thought, one anathema to the dominant ideologies of contemporary life that continually remind us, as a sticker on a car bumper recently did for me in perhaps unintentionally ironic terms, that 'family is the most important thing in life'. There is a bravery to Little Edie's being able to assert that the institution of the family is where she met the most grief in her long and remarkable life and, indeed, much of the fascination of *Grey Gardens* stems from the revelations it offers of two women expressing their indifference – and sometimes outright hostility – to the experiences of being Bouviers.

In this regard, *Grey Gardens* offers the first hybrid of two seemingly disparate cultural and cinematic forms: the melodrama and the documentary. The former had largely been the province of fiction film and television and has been characterised by its critics as concerned with domesticity, femininity, sexuality, maternalism and psychology, while the latter was, prior to this film, seen as concerned with ethnography, natural phenomenon, human public, social and institutional life. As discussed in the introduction, the most widely celebrated non-fiction films by D. A. Pennebaker, Richard Leacock, Frederick Wiseman and Albert and David Maysles were unconcerned with the private spaces of the household, with the lives of women and with the family. *Grey Gardens* moved the direct cinema camera into the space of the home and the family in a way previously unseen, and in order to organise its raw materials, it edited the Beales' commentaries into a generational conflict between mother and daughter – a building block of nearly all melodrama. In this regard, the household of Grey Gardens repeats the concerns of the melodrama in its fictional iterations by understanding the private sphere as shaped by larger forces of sexual desire, reproduction, social duty and sacrifice, and the gendered labour of maintaining the household – all clearly at work in the Beales' lives. Simultaneously, the film defies the constraints of the melodrama in at least one fundamental way: the mother refuses to see her relation to her daughter as solely one of sacrifice – a trope of the melodrama – and indeed defines herself as having given her daughter her freedom from the bonds of marriage, child-bearing and rearing, and household drudgery. In this regard, part of the film's appeal is that, though they never use the name, the Beales emerge within the film as icons of sex/gender defiance.

Marcia Landy describes melodrama – a genre that encompasses a variety of media forms and genres such as live theatre, cinema, television, literature and popular fiction – as:

driven by the experience of one crisis after another, crises involving severed familial ties, separation and loss, misrecognition of one's place, person and propriety. Seduction, betrayal, abandonment, extortion, murder, suicide, revenge, jealousy, incurable illness, obsession and compulsion – these are part of the familiar terrain of melodrama. The victims are most often females threatened in their sexuality, their property, their very identity. Often orphaned, subjected to cruel and arbitrary treatment at the hands of domineering paternal and maternal figures or their surrogates, they experience a number of trials, until, if they are fortunate, they are rescued by a gentle and understanding lover, the 'happy, unhappy ending' in Douglas Sirk's terms.[6]

This summation of the melodrama emphasises several key points which help to organise our understanding of the melodramatic appeal of *Grey Gardens*: first, that the phrase of 'the *familiar* terrain' of the melodrama underscores the family as the social body that defines the form; second, that the melodrama loves excess: crises, drama and performative exaggeration are at its heart – the slightly redacted phrase 'drama queen' gives us some inkling of the sense in which the melodrama has historically been seen as a less-than-subtle cultural product and its adherents as embracing the vulgar and over-blown. Third, the experiences of women shape the melodrama, not least the manner in which female sexuality is represented as giving rise to the crises that Landy articulates above – in this regard, female sexual desire inhabits a contradiction within the melodrama, one where women's desires appear as both a problem to be solved by the melodramatic plot *and* as a 'mystery' that is never resolved. Indeed, more often than not, the female protagonist's desire is largely disruptive of the domestic tranquility that always seems to reside just-out-of-reach for the melodrama. In short, the melodrama seems to want to explain the lives of women – characterised as they are by labour, domesticity, consumption, sexuality, marriage and children – but often seeks to want not so much to explain as to contain and control women's sexuality.

Taken together, these three features of the melodrama, as it is more generally understood, shape *Grey Gardens* and, were it a feature fiction film (which, in the course of time, it becomes in the form of the 2009 HBO production) the narrative of *Grey Gardens* would probably be unremarkable. It is *not* a fictional narrative, though, but instead one produced under the conditions of the Maysleses' ideals about the possibilities and practices of the direct cinema movement, and this fact suggests that part of the film's longstanding appeal and its popular resurgence in the past decade should be attributed to the sense that *Grey Gardens* heralds the moment in which the non-fiction film moves into the terrain of the melodrama and discovers rich materials that had previously been ignored by the documentary camera's lens. That is, the Maysleses discovered that melodrama is not solely a form of cultural production but a way of life as well.

The seemingly long delay in the arrival of the non-fiction film into the concerns of the melodrama makes a certain sense if we consider how the melodrama is, paradoxically, a deeply privatised cultural form. By this, I mean that melodramas are about family bonds, the private knowledge of the household and the sense that what most motivates the action of the melodrama is also what is most repressed; secrets and their revelations fuel melodramas, and while the non-fiction film would seem to find robust materials in the structure of the family, the question emerges: whose family? Whose family would reveal their grief, their joy, their petty grudges, their sorrow, their eccentricities and their downright madness before the non-fiction camera?

Living as we do in a world of non-fiction media such as reality programming that ceaselessly prompts disclosures about our ostensible 'private' lives, we, as audience members for the film, might not find *Grey Gardens* to be as provocative as it once was, but worth remembering is that the Beales seem to be among the earliest participants to allow a non-fiction film-maker to discover the inner workings of the household. In this regard, the status of the family, the importance of crisis and performance, and the role of female desire within the melodrama are all constituted in particular ways that meld the concerns of the melodrama with the needs of the direct cinema camera, and it is worth dwelling upon the specific manner in which the Maysleses and the film's editors, Hovde, Meyer and Froemke, shape the raw footage that they record of the Beales' performances while simultaneously we consider how the Beales are enacting melodrama for the Maysleses – and for us, as well.

For example, if the institution of the family and the stories its members tell about it organise the melodrama, we should ask about how the Maysleses' camera and microphone prompt and structure the Edies' commentary about their domestic lives. A crucial and

representative moment in the film for exploration of this question would be the notorious sequence in which we see a shot in which one of the household's many pet cats peers out from behind a portrait of Big Edie; the painting sits on the floor and is propped against the wall, and it emerges from the conversation that the pet is defecating on the floor of the women's shared bedroom. The audience overhears the conversation between the two Edies:

BIG EDIE   The cat's going to the bathroom right in back of my portrait.
LITTLE EDIE   God, isn't that awful?
BIG EDIE   No, I'm glad he is. I'm glad somebody's doing something he wanted to do.

This fleeting moment deserves our attention, if only because it frequently sponsors gasps and laughter in first-time viewers of the film; it is a signal moment about the squalor within the household and the apparent indifference of the two women to the level of dissolution at work in their personal lives and private space. Of particular interest is the fact that, while Big Edie is calling attention to the fact that their pets openly use the house as one large dumping-ground, Little Edie's interjection – 'God, isn't that awful?' – seems meant not for her mother so much as it is intended for the film-makers and the audience. Here, Little Edie gestures towards the fact that she recognises how more customary notions of household cleanliness and order would forbid such lax upkeep, and in this regard her comment installs David and Albert Maysles as stand-ins for a larger audience who might be – and often are – alarmed by this turn of events. The significant turn for the melodrama here is that one of its participants seeks to recognise the audience in a way that no fiction film heroine ever could, and she does so by making the film-makers into the proxy audience for her interactions with her mother.

Further, Big Edie can hardly be surprised by what is going on (and household visitors of the period record similar accounts of the shock of the odour of the house, laden with cat urine and other household refuse – a condition that Kristine McKenna describes succinctly as 'an unsanitary state of enchantment').[7] Her response to Little Edie's disgust only serves to intensify the sense of how her happiness derives from outright ignoring of domestic order and more usual notions of hygiene. Big Edie's remark about finding pleasure in someone else's ability to do as they like – 'I'm glad somebody's doing something he wanted to do' – is as important a vindication for how she has lived her life for the past four decades as any in the film, given that it reminds us that, at least as Big Edie sees it, one is never granted permission to live as one likes. A person must simply live as such. Her comment – a seeming throw-away line in a domestic conversation – reveals the theatricality through which the Edies lived their lives and inhabits the melodramatic dimensions of the everyday, where a gesture or comment is both unimportant in the large scheme of things and yet also immensely significant for disclosing the state of mind of the person who offers it.

The melodrama in fact emphasises this combination of the mundane and the over-the-top and has done so historically for a long time; Peter Brooks argues that the 'hyperbolic set of gestures' that we discover in melodramas emerges in the early nineteenth century because in the melodrama, Brooks tells us, 'things cease to be merely themselves, gestures cease to be merely tokens of social intercourse whose meaning is assigned by the social code'.[8] Objects and gestures in melodramas express the thoughts and feelings of the characters and the social tensions between those characters – they 'act out', as it were – because those characters seem unable to say what it is that is really on their minds in direct and explicit fashion. To speak so directly and so bluntly would risk too much – risk speaking of the contradictions and antagonisms that always reside within the household, and indeed are probably created and fostered by domestic life to begin with.

It should come as little surprise, then, that the two Edies see the capacity to sing and to dance as the source of their antagonism to the larger Bouvier family *and* simultaneously as the consolation for their exile from the family for that very same inclination to perform. Little Edie comments in an interview with journalist Kristine McKenna after her mother's death, for example, that

the family never cared for me and they hated my mother. She was a dancer and singer with a terrific voice she'd inherited from her mother, and the relatives hated her because she was magnificent. She had no interest in the social clubs and bridge games her family was involved with.[9]

The version of events that Little Edie reports here is not that she and her mother were exiled from their family because of her mother's divorce, but that the marriage failed because her mother had talents that could not be contained or usefully constrained within the strictures of marriage and child-rearing and, as noted above, she would never receive permission to express those talents but would have to grant such to herself. Telling in Little Edie's comment to

McKenna is her sense that femininity within the Bouviers was characterised by the impulse to sing and to dance – her grandmother, Little Edie suggests, passed it to her daughter and her daughter extended the gift, the gift to be 'magnificent'. I would argue that Little Edie is emphasising the sense that singing and dancing allowed her mother and herself (and her grandmother, as well) to 'act out' upon the pressures they experienced to be conventional and to conform to familial expectations, but that such impulses carried with them larger penalties – especially for her mother – than any of them could predict.

Such performances are not restricted, I would suggest, to the Beales themselves but extend to the house of Grey Gardens itself, and the sense that the mansion becomes a character within the film is not as outlandish as it might seem. Many critics of the melodrama have noted that the physical objects that appear in the spaces depicted take on additional meanings beyond that solely of utility; thus, a kitchen is not solely the space of food preparation but also can become associated with the claustrophobia of domesticity or the pleasures of familial interaction. Later on, I discuss how Little Edie's fashions become a central aspect of *Grey Gardens*' visual impact, but here I would underscore the sense that the house itself conveys much information and insight into the lives of the Beales, emphasising its presence as what John David Rhodes describes as a 'hybrid of the commonplace and the fantastic'.[10] By this, Rhodes asks us to consider how the access to the house that the Beales give to the Maysleses, and by turns the Maysleses give to us, organises our responses to the Beales as we see, on the one hand, them engaged in the drudgery of everyday life – and especially a life of material poverty – and, on the other hand, the outlandish and playful aspects of their lives. The house itself participates in this because it performs an important function for the camera; as Rhodes tells us in his reading of the film's opening sequence, the first shot in the film is from the house's point of view. That is, the audience's first glimpse is not from the outside of the house but from its interior, as we overhear the Edies conversing about

a lost cat and welcoming the Maysleses into their home. It is as if Grey
Gardens inaugurates the film *Grey Gardens* and participates in the
crises and performances that inhere to its melodrama.

The melodramatic aspects of the film's *mise en scène* thus derive
from the uncanny sense that the house itself is a character in the film,
and this idea allows us to understand how the house's affective pull
on its inhabitants and on the viewers produces strong emotional
responses. Perhaps this is one reason why viewers of *Grey Gardens*
often articulate a response of fascinated horror. The film sponsors a
strong affective response that both encourages a scopophilic pleasure
in the manner by which the Maysleses give the film's audience access
to scenes of domestic privacy and its performances and a sense that
the film's viewers often feel 'trapped' within the events and their
filming to such a degree that is evocative, I would argue, for many
viewers about the experiences they share of home-life and its
emotional demands. Some people with whom I have talked about the
film have gone so far as to tell me that they could not watch the film

in its entirety because its depictions of the two Edies' conversations evoked similar familial bonds, ones that they loathed to have recalled for them. *Grey Gardens* inspires strong reactions in it viewers, not all of them positive and many of them characterised by disgust, fear and helplessness.

In a culture so abundantly furnished with evocations of violence and disharmony as our own, it is no small thing, then, to achieve the kind of affective response that *Grey Gardens* makes possible, all done simply by recording the conversations of two women who, for most purposes, seemed to have enjoyed a deeply loving and nurturing bond. Given that *Grey Gardens* has no music track – a nearly universal accessory to the visual culture of horror – and no special effects, this dimension of the film might puzzle us. What exactly are they saying and doing that might prompt such anxiety, dread and longing in some of the film's viewers?

The film's capacity to sponsor feelings of claustrophobia probably is easiest to explore, given that the bulk of *Grey Gardens* takes place in one room, *the* one room that the Edies seemed to inhabit: their bedroom. This space – painted a vivid yellow, and furnished with two single beds – is the scene of almost every conversation between them, and not solely for the practical reason that Big Edie maintained a limited physical mobility and for most of the film is witnessed sitting or lying on her bed. The near-minimal household finances have distilled the Edies' domestic life so that almost everything happens in this room – cooking (on a hot-plate on Big Edie's bed), eating (often from a small refrigerator), reading, listening to the radio and vinyl records, receiving their few guests. Given that the Edies' scant financial resources have required them to sell almost all the furniture in the household (and the fact that the central heating was a luxury in a twenty-eight-room house, one designed to be maintained by servants), practical necessity, in part, drove them to inhabit this small space within the larger house.

The utility of their shared domestic space, though, only goes part way to understanding the sense of claustrophobic enclosure that

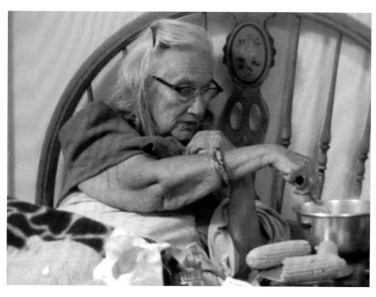

the film brings about in viewers and the containment within the room is not solely physical but psychic as well. It is not just the fact that there seems nowhere else in the house to which to retreat, but that there is no other social relation within grasp beyond that of the familial. More to the point, the familial here is distilled to its most concentrated essence, the parent and the child, and even more pointedly to the bond between mother and daughter. Indeed, beyond the few visitors whom we witness – Gerry, the young handyman; Lois and John, the guests at Big Edie's birthday party; the Maysleses themselves – the only other figures within the house are the images of the two women themselves, rendered in oil portraits, sketches, fashion photography and newspaper clippings. Grey Gardens is inhabited not only by the Edies but also by the historical documents of the bond between them, and one way of interpreting the film is to understand it as the conversation that families often have about themselves around their accumulated archives of photographs and related materials. Making matters more compelling is that this conversation occurs between two women, women whose lives have been shaped by their resistance to conventional notions of marriage and child-rearing as those practices define women's experiences of the family within patriarchy.

Of course, this familial feminine conversation is not necessarily one of agreement or consensus, and indeed the differences between how parents and children narrate the past is frequently the source of dispute and rancour. In this light, *Grey Gardens* reveals the allure of witnessing familial conversations that are *not* our own. We need not be absolutely convinced of the relevance of the psychoanalytic account of the family to learn from Sigmund Freud's writings on the topic, not least about how the relations between parents and children frequently bring about in the child, at least according to Freud, a desire to narrate the circumstances through which he or she came to be as they are. Furthermore, this desire to narrate the events of his/her birth and maturation can take on a fantastic dimension, one that Freud referred to as the 'familienroman' and that is translated most often into English as the 'family romance' but whose more literal meaning in the original German is closer to 'story' or 'novel'. *Grey Gardens*, in the language of psychoanalysis, takes the form of Little Edie's family romance – that is, the fantasy that Freud claims a child needs about her parents in order to explain her own life.

This fantasy, according to Freud, stems from the child's eventual and necessary discovery that he or she must share the attention and affections of the parents with a larger world, not least with siblings but also with other people more generally, and the demand to relinquish the idea that the parents exist solely for the child can foster in him/her the idea that the parents do not love the child as lavishly as they ought – at least according to the child. This discovery, according to Freud, makes the child resentful and such resentment can sponsor fantasies that the reason the parents fail to love the child adequately is that it is not the love of the child's 'real' parents – that the child has been somehow mistakenly trapped with imposters. Compounding matters is the sense that, as the child matures, he or she discovers that the idealistic version of the parents that has been nurtured within the seclusion of the household is giving way to a sense of other possibilities of how to live, more specifically that there are others outside the household for whom the parents might have affection.

The 'family novel' of the child emerges, as Freud writes, 'in the idea, often consciously recollected later from early childhood, of being a step-child or an adopted child'. After having asserted the idea that one's parents are in fact *not* one's actual parents, the child's fantasy can elaborate both the denigrated status of one's actual (read: inauthentic) parents (i.e., they are not worthy of the child's love) and make the child's 'real' (and ostensibly lost) parents into heroes who are looking for their lost child. These fantastic assertions on behalf of the child have unexpected consequences, not least that the child feels superior to the domestic life around her, but also that she needs that domestic life to nurture her sense that she really ought to be somewhere else with the 'real' family that is lost to her.

Of particular interest for us is the fact that Freud sees these wishes and feelings as most intensely felt by children towards the parent of the same sex, and that part of the child's fantasy 'tends to picture to himself erotic situations and relations, the motive force behind this being his desire to bring [the] mother (who is the subject of the most intense sexual curiosity) into situations of secret infidelity and into secret love-affairs'.[11] The sum of Freud's description of this narrative as it is invented by the child, and especially the female child, is that the child – even as an adult – will seek to explain how she developed into the woman she is as a result of her mother's love for a man who is not her father; put another way, the daughter explains her situation as the outcome of the mother's illicit sexual and romantic bonds with men outside of her marriage. Freud deems this fantasy about the mother as a form of 'revenge and retaliation' by children who 'were punished by their parents for sexual naughtiness and who now revenge themselves on their parents by means of phantasies of this kind'.[12]

It comes as little surprise, then, that Big Edie and Little Edie are depicted within *Grey Gardens* as engaged in extensive narration and counter-narration of each other's relations to men and, in this regard, perhaps what we sense about the claustrophobic dimensions of the film is the possibility that their affection centres around an agreed-upon capacity to fantasise – both by the mother and the daughter – about each other's love lives. Further, they are each licensed by the other to fantasise and speculate upon the meanings of the other's romantic and erotic liaisons, but only with the understanding that these events are rooted firmly in the past (although, as is discussed below, Little Edie sees her interactions with the film-makers as the opportunity to re-enact these fantasies anew). Freud's account comes up short in regards to the Beales' bond because they have reversed the agency of the fantasy in that the daughter is mandated to speculate openly about the mother's relations to men who are not the father. What does persist from Freud's accounts is the question of whether vengefulness remains a part of Little Edie's motivation, and I would argue that it does.

But, a new complication arises: Big Edie seems to have installed her extra-marital bonds as part of the conversation, thus depriving Little Edie of the means through which to secure the revenge upon her mother that Freud thought to be the child's compensation for having conceded the parent's love. Thus, the task of discussing Big Edie's relations to men other than Phelan Beale seems more of a chore than anything else for Little Edie and, in that regard, her comments on the matter emerge more as a put-down of her mother than a fantasy. Put more bluntly: how exciting can it be to fantasise about a parent's erotic partnerings when that task has been assigned to the child by the parent? How does one enliven this chore?

Little Edie must gain her revenge in another manner and her solution is to see both her mother's marriage and her extra-marital relations as failures – but of different kinds. Regarding the former, in a conversation over family photographs from Big Edie's early marriage and Little Edie's childhood, Little Edie reads aloud for the camera an inscription from her father to her mother written by him on his own portrait; Phelan Beale's dedication reads: 'To my best friend and most delightful comrade; to my only sweetheart and wonderful wife, I tender the likeness of her husband.' Little Edie, in a mocking tone, interprets this as an ironic commentary on the failure of their marriage, but Big Edie counters that 'I lived alone these thirty years; I didn't mind it. You get very independent,' and that 'I've had a very happy, very satisfying life.' Little Edie responds by asserting that 'You had a rich husband. You should have stayed with him. You might as well face it.' Big Edie's subsequent conclusion is to see her reclusion to Grey Gardens for the past three decades not as the result of the end of her marriage but as a deliberate choice to devote herself to her art, and more specifically her singing. 'I had a terribly successful marriage. I came down to live in this house because I did all my singing here,' she comments, as if to thwart her daughter's insistence that the marriage failed because Phelan treated his wife – at least, according to his note on the photograph – as more like a school chum than a wife.

If the two women interpret the meanings of Big Edie's marriage in starkly different terms, they maintain a more ambiguous agreement about the nature of the mother's relation to her music and, by implication, the man most vividly identified with it, George Strong. Strong, or 'Gould' as he is referred to in the film, is described by both women as Big Edie's 'accompanist' and the proof of the relation is seen, or more properly, is heard on the recordings made by Big Edie and Gould, which are played by Little Edie on a small record player for the film-makers. This sequence appears after the two women have argued over whether the elder's life and marriage have been happy; Little Edie's response to her mother's perception of a happy marriage is to remind Big Edie, via a sound recording, that her singing centred upon her relation to Gould. Thus, when we see Little Edie playing the particular song whose title is 'We Belong Together', she uses the record to ventriloquise an indictment of her mother's fantasy of a perfect marriage by indirectly reminding her – and announcing to the film-makers and the audience – that, counter to Phelan's stilted and chilly dedication on the photograph, Big Edie recorded, literally, her desire for Gould on the records that Little Edie plays.

It is at this moment that Albert Maysles' camera is overly burdened with attempting to fix both women's expressions as they respond to the awkward presence of Big Edie's singing her devotion to a man she has just described not only as 'brilliant' but as, in fact, 'more intelligent' than her husband. It is at this moment that Little Edie gazes deliberately and awkwardly away from her mother; she grins with satisfaction that the record is proving her point about her mother's fantasy about her marriage and shoots a glance to the camera as if to confirm her being right. Big Edie, by contrast, sheepishly smiles with both pleasure at hearing the confidence in her recorded voice and with the awkwardness at knowing that her relation to Gould seems to be emerging as more than just that of singer and pianist. She coyly adjusts the brim of the hat she wears and mouths the words in synch with her recorded voice as if to

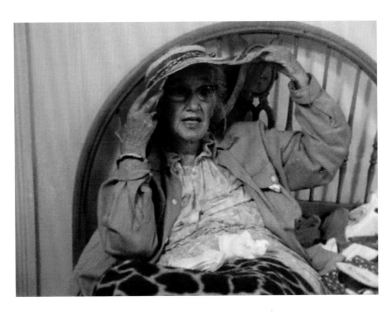

pretend that the unfortunate fact of her relation to Gould – as it relates to her separation from Phelan – is hardly the matter at hand.

The conversation that follows is one of the central ones of the film in that each of them begins to recognise that they are not solely discussing Big Edie's relation to Gould – that the topic under discussion in fact is emerging to be the reason they have found themselves reduced to the poverty and social exile in which they live. Each discloses their understanding of why they have spent the past years secluded in their house:

BIG EDIE	My mother gave me the right slant on my voice. She told me to leave everything.
LITTLE EDIE	No man could compete against Mrs Beale and Gould. No man in the world.
BIG EDIE	Well, I worked hard.
LITTLE EDIE [to camera]	How could she be bothered with anything in the world when she had a talent like that?

BIG EDIE	I had to take care of this house, I lived on no money.
LITTLE EDIE	You were able to save the house on account of me.
BIG EDIE:	Yeah. ...
LITTLE EDIE	I didn't want to live in Easthampton but I had to on account of mother's house.
BIG EDIE	Well, now you see why you lived, because you had music all the time. And, you went to the beach, too. That's what you like.
LITTLE EDIE	Well. ...
BIG EDIE	I think you liked your dancing. You were very good at that. [We then hear the non-vocal musical arrangement for 'Tea for Two', which Big Edie sings.]

Remarkable about this exchange is Big Edie's clear-headed assertion that she is satisfied with the sacrifices that she has made for her art and that, indeed, the squalor that surrounds them is the price she has paid for not neglecting her talent. If, as she comments, her mother told her 'to leave everything' for her singing, then in her mind that is what she has done and she appears to have no regrets about these choices. Little Edie, by contrast, expresses an ambivalence about the choices her mother has made; for her, it was necessary for her to return to Grey Gardens in order not just to 'save the house', but in order to allow her mother to live – not to make music, but to *survive*. Her misgivings about this turn of events – the exchange of her freedom as a young woman in New York for her mother's ability to stay at Grey Gardens – are tempered by the sense that she seems genuinely to respect Big Edie's talents and to understand that, even for women of their social privilege and wealth, their singing and dancing were priorities only for them and, more to point, were seen by others as distractions from their ostensibly more important obligations to marry and to have children.

Thus, as if to ameliorate the effects of this discovery – the fact that her mother's relation to Gould had a greater significance than that to her own father – Little Edie reverses herself, leaving behind the smirking and ironic tone through which she just previously implied that her mother's fantasies of success and happiness were a sham and, with a poignant, side-long glance to the camera, murmurs that 'no man could compete against Mrs Beale and Gould'. With this comment, Little Edie embraces her mother's need for a bond outside her marriage – with her art and with Gould and confirms that her mother's need to sing was more important than that of maintaining a family and a household. More ambiguous, though, is the sense in Little Edie's comment that *no man* could compete against the pairing of her mother and Gould, rendering the latter pairing as feminised against any specific man. Little Edie's remark invests the household with a femininity that all men in general are seen as antagonistic towards, including the Maysleses themselves.

At this moment, an affective economy at the heart of the household begins to emerge within the film, an economy that requires the Edies to accept the following terms: they may pursue their art by rejecting conventional bonds to men, but the costs of this rejection will be high and will risk mental and physical deprivation. They will have lost their ties to the social world in which they have lived, and will sense that the smallest of infractions will be penalised – when Little Edie jokes, after the 'raid' by the health authorities, that 'they can get you for anything in Easthampton – they can get you for wearing red shoes on a Thursday', the joke reveals her grief and despair over the ostracisation through which she and her mother have come to live their lives. As we will learn in the next chapter, though, Little Edie's joke about fashion here contains within it a serious commitment on her part to living outside the conventions of social life, not least dress and clothing among them.

2 'The Revolutionary Costume': Little Edie and Fashion

My costumes? That's a protest against having worked as a model for the establishment, believe it or not. A lot of models feel that way. Sometimes their lives are protests against having worked as models. Besides, I didn't have time taking care of mother to get out and buy any clothes. So I used what was left of mine and mother's in the attic.

Little Edie Beale

The previous chapter argued that the house in *Grey Gardens* is a character in this melodrama. If this is true, then Little Edie is its star, and she consistently dresses for the part. Indeed, perhaps the most cited aspect of *Grey Gardens*' *mise en scène* is Little Edie's physical appearance and deportment. At different moments, she wears ensembles of clothing, jewellery, bath-towels and scarves composed out of various garments that she repurposes: a skirt becomes a turban, a blouse becomes a skirt, a swimsuit becomes an evening dress. In a key moment of the film, she describes the clothing she is wearing as 'the revolutionary costume', and suggests that the larger world is not yet ready for it – that is, she only wears this clothing when she is at home because of the scorn and rejection she might experience from being seen in public in her inventions. She confesses her thoughts about her appearance to the Maysleses in a hushed and conspiratorial tone outside the house and well away from any other listeners. She comments:

This is the best thing to wear for today, you understand. Because I don't like women in skirts and the best thing is to wear pantyhose or some pants under a short skirt, I think. Then you have the pants under the skirt and then you can pull the stockings up over the pants underneath the skirt. And you can

always take off the skirt and use it as a cape. So I think this is the best costume for today.

We might recall that, in 1973, a cape as a functioning part of a woman's wardrobe was by that point outré, and in this regard the versatility that Little Edie attributes to her wardrobe derives, at least within these comments, from her sense of utility: rather than approach the idea of fashion from its luxury, pleasure and social status, Little Edie seems to be thinking of her clothing as something that adapts to the conditions of daily life (albeit, her own, perhaps peculiar daily life) – weather, social encounters, activities of labour and leisure. Tellingly, though, the language of 'costumes' that she uses here reveals that she understands all too well the theatricality of her appearance – costumes are for performances, and she designs her looks in the film to augment her gestures, her words and her own gaze upon others around her.

Her comments omit what might seem to be the most obvious aspect of her relation to clothing and to fashion: namely, she does not acknowledge that she organises her clothing in order to be looked at. I would argue that, despite her failing to do so, she aligns two disparate activities that are at the heart of women's relation to fashion in the modern era, namely that she understands herself as someone who seeks to earn the attention of others through her appearance – this is not the same thing as conventional social status – and she sees herself remotely: that is, she is intensely aware of the effect that her appearance has upon others because she can look, so to speak, through their eyes.

This, of course, might be described more generally as the situation that all women find themselves in, especially within a social order derived from men's privileged gazes over women, but Little Edie's biography tells us two important and exceptional things about how she experienced her presence as a woman within this more general tendency. First, her childhood, adolescence and young adulthood were lived with a beautiful and expensive wardrobe

commensurate with the wealth to which she was accustomed. Her own collection of photographs from her infancy to the 1940s confirms this – she enjoyed beautiful clothing and she knew how to wear it. Second, and most pertinently for a discussion of her presence in *Grey Gardens*, she knew how to pose in her wardrobe for the camera. Her published photographic album[13] includes images of her in a range of garments that includes swimwear, trousers, day dresses, furs and evening wear, and the kinds of photographs in which we see her tell us that she was comfortable in front of the camera from an early age. Studio portraits, snapshots, images from fashion shows and weddings, all suggest an experience of the world in which her appearance as a beautiful, well-dressed and well-groomed young woman was assumed as the index of her status as a subject of privilege. Her papers confirm this; among her correspondence is a 14 January 1936 letter from the Publicity Department of the R. H. Macy department store asking her to consider modelling for them; as the author writes 'nearly everyone who has seen your pictures here thinks you are the lovliest [sic]'.

It is all the more remarkable, then, that when the Maysleses arrived in the early 1970s, Little Edie had spent the previous two decades hidden from the world and increasingly was wearing a wardrobe that she had, by necessity, repurposed for her own ends. Her life, then, can be divided into two periods: the first three and a half decades in the trappings of public glamour and visible wealth, and the following two decades in private squalor and hidden poverty.

Yet, she seems almost instinctively to have known how to engage the Maysleses' camera, as if the previous two decades had not occurred, and perhaps viewers find her presence in the film to be so compelling because she appears – literally – to be unaware that the relation she has to herself and to others through her body and through fashion is more appropriate to the role a younger woman is expected to inhabit. Put another way, Little Edie's twenty years of privation before the making of the film have prevented her from aging in the more customary manner, where her sense of herself might increasingly be divorced from her embrace of her physical presence and the delight she takes in clothing. Her allure derives from the unanticipated discovery that she does not obey the demands of the fashion and culture industries to abandon those ostensibly youthful delights in the corporeal and the sartorial.

Conjoined with its fascinations with the melodrama, then, *Grey Gardens* discovers fashion and costuming as part of the unexpected world that the Beales have made for themselves and, if feminine spectacle is a key element of the fiction film in the production of stardom, then *Grey Gardens*' film-makers make a star out of Little Edie. This is a significant aspect of the film's remobilisation in recent projects and in fan commentary, and, in this regard, I would argue that *Grey Gardens*' appeal coincided with the emerging popularisation of fashion as self-invention and the sense that it was idiosyncratic personal style, financial necessity and a defiant playfulness that organised Little Edie's appearance.

As audience interest in the film has expanded since its release, the visual culture of photographs, letters and paraphernalia related to the film has equally become more expansive; one of the most significant projects to appear in this vein is a volume edited by members of the Beales family after Little Edie's death which contains a range of media from her personal archive. This collection offers an astonishing wealth of materials for making sense of the film, and for a discussion of the film's relation to fashion, two particular photographs of the Edies[14] serve as poignant traces of the life that mother and daughter shared and the tolls that their increasing poverty over the decades took on them.

The earlier photo is undated but would seem to be from around 1940; Little Edie appears to be a young woman, perhaps twenty or so years of age. She stands beside her mother and wears a sleeveless A-line dress of calico and batik with a necklace of large beads. Her hair is on her shoulders and she smiles demurely. The second photograph, from 1962, depicts them approximately twenty years later and, again, Little Edie wears the same dress. It has been recut –

the cap sleeves of the bodice have been removed and tailored into a halter, while the skirt is shorter and now is worn over a fuller circle skirt of a dark, solid colour. She wears no jewellery, but in this photo her head is wrapped in a scarf in what would become her signature style.

Each photograph shows the two women's different relation to fashion, not least because Big Edie seems drab when standing next to her daughter; in each image, Big Edie seems slump-shouldered and matronly, while her daughter brings herself to the camera with an awareness of how to have her elegant and composed figure captured on film. The years have clearly taken their toll, and yet Little Edie wears the same dress and, truth be told, has maintained the figure for it. In the later photograph, though, their faces offer a sadness that tells of the deprivations of their household. This pairing of photos also tells of the importance, though, of appearances and the pleasures of clothing and deportment that offered comfort, especially to Little Edie, during difficult times. While it is tempting to describe this comfort as 'fashion', that name does not quite fit with what we witness of Little Edie's relation to clothing, her body and the roles that those things played over the course of her life: fashion would imply that she always was able to keep up with trends and fads in clothing, but this seems to have been true only for the first part of her life – after that, she seems to have become increasingly 'unfashionable' but, paradoxically, more capable of shaping her appearance in inventive and striking ways.

The immense renewed interest by audiences in *Grey Gardens* in the past decade emerges in large part around Little Edie's relation to fashion and to her own unfashionableness because she does two seemingly contradictory things simultaneously. First, she unembarrassedly embraces clothing and takes pleasure in her appearance while, second, she does so with apparently little financial support for such or access to the marketplaces of fashion. Further, she inhabits this tension by inventing her own unique look, marked as it is by a playful repurposing of clothing and, more to the point, a

willingness to make her ostensible shortcomings into her most noticeable features. The manner in which Little Edie lives within this bind – of loving fashion and having no money – would seem to be an untenable one, to the degree that fashion as it is so often lived in contemporary life encourages each consumer to appear wealthier than he/she is – what marketing and publicity discourses describe as its 'aspirational' dimensions. What Little Edie aspires to in her wardrobe is not entirely clear, but given that she wears a bath-towel as a turban, it would seem to be something beyond the more conventional notions of good taste and propriety that were on offer in 1973.

Complicating this is her age and her hair-loss; during the summer in which *Grey Gardens* was shot, Little Edie was fifty-five years old and her hair was both going grey and going away. While she seems never to have offered an explanation for the loss of her hair – and by all accounts, she had lost a lot of it – her choice to cover it with all manner of scarves, towels, turbans and hats allowed her to use her coiffeur as an extension of the playful technique she brought to her wardrobe more generally. This is not to make light of her predicament, inasmuch as the loss of her hair might have been a symptom of ill health and indeed could only have been made worse by the emotional and financial pressures under which she and her mother lived. But, if Andy Warhol is right when he suggests that 'you should point out all your beauty problems and defects right away, rather than take a chance [that other people] won't notice them',[15] then Little Edie has learned to orchestrate her appearance around all of her ostensible 'beauty problems', as Warhol might call them, not least her poverty and the loss of her hair.

The relation between *Grey Gardens* and the films of Andy Warhol, another important non-fiction project of the 1960s beyond that of the direct cinema movement, is an important one, if only because the Edies would have seemed, had they been able and willing to leave the confines of their house, ideal subjects for the films that Warhol had produced throughout the 1960s. Central to Warhol's film-making, for example, was the idea of everyday stardom. By this, his films underscore the glamorous appeal of the Hollywood studio film as it had become part of the lives of spectators; many of the performers in Warhol's cinema frequently sought to enact themselves as the stars of their own lives, and in the production of his films Warhol sought out eccentric and flamboyant figures of New York City's various demimonde subcultures of the period: artists, actors, musicians, writers, debutantes, hangers-on, druggies, drop-outs and all manner of people who saw themselves as ready for the embrace of the glamourising camera. Indeed, it was another Edie – a Sedgwick, in this case – who imported her own wounded-girl appeal to Warhol's cinema of the period and who, like many others, received little instruction or direction beyond that of simply being themselves in front of the lens. Edie Sedgwick, who performed in Warhol vehicles such as *Vinyl*, *Poor Little Rich Girl* and *Beauty No. 2*, embodied the aesthetic of the moment and as such can be seen as preparatory to the effect that Big Edie and Little Edie had upon their audiences.

The parallel between *Grey Gardens* and Warhol's 'underground' cinema of the 1960s extends beyond the performative exaggeration which Warhol nurtured in his actors – and which keys audiences of *Grey Gardens* to the appeal of the Beales – to the gender play which Warhol depicted in his films. One name for this play is drag, and framing the Beales' performances in terms of drag brings into focus the sense that they are enacting versions of themselves and of a femininity that seems a relic of a prior historical moment. Warhol himself commented that:

drag queens are living testimony to the way women used to be, the way some people still want them to be, and the way some women will actually want to be. Drags are ambulatory archives of ideal moviestar womanhood. They perform a documentary service, usually consecrating their lives to keeping the glittering alternative alive and available for (not-too-close) inspection.[16]

Warhol's use of the term 'documentary' here resonates with *Grey Gardens*' framing of Little Edie's appearance and, in particular, the sense that, as non-fiction film, it resituates 'moviestar womanhood' from the fantasy life of the spectator to the moving image itself. In other words, the allure of *Grey Gardens* is similar to that of the underground film: it shows a world in which the Hollywood product organises the lives of its viewers, viewers who in turn take over the film frame.

The differences between the glamorous Hollywood image and what spectators can achieve in their efforts to emulate it fascinate us because we are pressed to note just how large the gulf between the two frequently is – poverty, fatigue, age, all take their toll on the individual who works to have a little 'moviestar womanhood'. Little Edie, with her grey hair peaking from beneath her turban, becomes an emblem of such disparity. The fact of her aging in this context allows us to see how an ageist culture visits its worst judgments upon women as they mature. Pamela Church Gibson describes the challenges posed to women as they age as the problem of becoming invisible within a culture industry that is organised around the idealisation of adolescence and young adulthood; she comments that many women during middle age and later have 'experienced a feeling of being unwelcome and have donned a sartorial cloak in order to suit their social invisibility'. In this regard, many women's lives become characterised by a sense of disappearing from the social sphere because of the devaluation of their appearance *and* by the sense that they nevertheless are forced to appear – the body cannot simply be made to become nothing. 'The majority of women in their sixties and upwards' cope with this situation, Church Gibson argues, in that they 'seem to be following their own sartorial rules', rules which make them stand out in comparison to younger women and simultaneously seem to produce a conformity among such women during and after middle age.[17] Church Gibson argues that this tendency to conform among women as they age reproduces a social dynamic pertinent to adolescents, and particularly young women, who seek inclusion among their peers by dwelling within narrow constraints of what is deemed acceptable clothing, makeup and hair.

I dwell on this predicament as Church Gibson offers it in order to consider the challenges met by Little Edie in the choices she makes about her clothing and her appearance because I think that a central appeal of *Grey Gardens* has been the manner in which it shows us a woman who encounters the problem that Church Gibson describes while, at the same time, she does not even have the benefit of the resources to shop for new clothing or the larger social group with which to commiserate over her age-based exile from fashion culture. Compounding matters is the fact that her relation to her mother fosters a sense of herself as a fashionable woman; the affective bond between the two women is often nurtured by Little Edie's manufacture of herself as a feminine spectacle – and Big Edie's matriarchal stature concurrently is affirmed by her disavowal of fashion.

Indeed, Big Edie's presence – bodily and affectively – challenges the claims we might make about eccentricity, mental health and

femininity as they surround her daughter. Although both Edies
dwelled in a world of wealth and access to fashion prior to the
poverty they encountered in their later years, no discussion of fashion
within the film can neglect the sense that Big Edie seems to have
become indifferent to clothing in a way that her daughter never does.
In a key scene early in the film, we see the Edies sun-bathing on a
porch elevated among the house's surrounding trees. Little Edie wears
a swimsuit, high-heeled pumps and her signature head-scarf, while
her mother wears a turtle-necked sweater wrapped across her breasts
and a towel beneath. As she begins to move from the rocking chair
on which she's been reclining, her clothing shifts and falls from her,
provoking an exchange with Little Edie:

LITTLE EDIE   Mother, you don't have enough clothes on.
BIG EDIE   Well, I'm going to get naked in just a minute, so you better
               watch out.
LITTLE EDIE   That's what I'm afraid of.

BIG EDIE	Yeah, for what, now why? I haven't got any warts on me.
LITTLE EDIE	But the movie, the movie!
BIG EDIE	I haven't got any warts on me!
LITTLE EDIE	That isn't the point, mother darling.

What *is* the point, though? The intention of Big Edie's warning ('you better watch out') remains unclear: she obviously is not afraid that her body is somehow contagious (with warts or any other agent) but knows that Little Edie is anxious about the possibility that her mother's body might be exposed for the camera. Such a possibility perhaps distresses Little Edie to the degree that her mother is not concerned with the prospect of exposure when, by contrast, the daughter endlessly occupies herself with covering, and especially covering her hair.

Grey Gardens' reception among audiences has long noted the way that clothing and fashion are at the heart of the film; as fashion designer Todd Oldham notes in a commentary bundled with the DVD version of *Grey Gardens*, the Maysleses' film was circulating among the New York design community when he first moved there in the mid-1980s and had already achieved a cult status for Little Edie's ensembles alone. Oldham remarks that Little Edie influenced his aesthetic for four reasons: her sense of colour, her sense of proportion, her playfulness in inventing and reusing garments for new and unforeseen reasons and, finally, her consistent personal style which seems to carry from ensemble to ensemble. Among Oldham's insights about the film is that this style carried over to her relation to the Maysleses themselves – Edie seems to have been seduced by the presence of the Maysleses and they in turn seem intrigued by the way that she consistently turns herself out for them, bringing a new look for each day they come to photograph.

Fellow-designer John Bartlett, also interviewed for the DVD and who has also created seasonal lines of his womens-wear inspired by Little Edie, emphasises the sense of play within Little Edie's sartorial aesthetic. For Bartlett, she seemed to obey no rules of what constitutes 'good taste' and saw clothing as the occasion to be creative in a life ruled by poverty and the dull grind of survival and, indeed, this sense of the ludic within the pathos of her limited resources emerges elsewhere in fan commentary on the film. The blogosphere has participated in this discourse; for example, blogger 'Sadie', who writes at thepetitesophisticate.blogspot.com and at Jezebel.com, devoted her remarks in the autumn of 2008, right after the global financial crash that unleashed the largest financial crisis in the United States since the Great Depression of the 1930s, to the topic of Little Edie's fashion as a model for the newly financially constrained. In a column titled, 'Little Edie Beale: The Ultimate Recessionista', from 10 November 2008, she writes

A couple of years ago, Little Edie Beale, the eccentric poor relation of Jackie Kennedy immortalized in *Grey Gardens*, was discovered by Fashion. We all know the trademarks: cashmere sweaters on her head, upside-down skirts, pantyhose sarongs, trouser minis. Designers were thrilled by this creativity, quick to reinvent and intellectualize it in expensive fabrics. But Little Edie wasn't intellectual; she was instinctive. With straitened circumstances and, okay, a healthy dash of delusion, she condensed a hundred *Today* show segments every hour. Reinvention? Check. Second-hand chic? Check. DIY? Natch. ... Little Edie, from madness or wisdom, didn't do that. She created a new reality for a new set of circumstances.[18]

According to Sadie, Little Edie becomes a more potent emblem of creativity-under-pressure for consumers who will experience a loss of purchasing power and access to the fashion commodity. Sadie then extends her comments upon the relation between Little Edie's eccentric fashion sense and her mental well-being; she notes that Simon Doonan, a well-known art director, had commented about a friend,

who works in a psychiatric hospital and has a front-row seat at the unwitting fashion show that is mental illness. 'Walk around any in-patient unit: Lots of people are sitting around with things tied around their heads, just like Little Edie. They are not making a fashion statement; they are trying to block out the voices in their heads.'[19]

This remark subsequently sponsors passionate responses among Sadie's readers because many of them think that Little Edie's relation to her body and to clothing is to be read as symptomatic of a distressing mental pathology and one that is not to be taken lightly. One respondent, topsyjane, comments that:

I couldn't make it through [the film] either. Between my own ongoing mental health problems and my close relationship with my mom, I can all too easily see myself sliding into this kind of life, minus the mansion at the beach, famous relatives, and interest from brilliant film-makers. I also hate the fetishizing of Little Edie's 'style' by the fashion insiders.[20]

In a similar manner, a respondent named raymi suggests that 'people who constantly change outfits throughout the day, mixing and matching prints that somehow turn out fabulous, are bipolar, and it stems from an obsessive need to be creative, always. It is an illness but not so terrible I think',[21] while 'southernbitch' offers that 'it was just a really uncomfortable line between campy and mental illness, and ultimately I didn't know if I felt like I was being informed or if I was perpetuating in an exploitation [sic]'.[22] Little Edie's appearance sponsors a discomfort worth dwelling upon if only because it offers a specific aspect of the film where we discover an immense divergence in the ways that viewers see the film's central figures: either as heroic or as pathetic.

Worth dwelling upon in southernbitch's comment is that one reading of the film would see it as encouraging its viewers to participate in the exploitation of these women, one that historically extends back to the way that Pauline Kael responded to the Maysleses' film projects in the 1960s, as discussed in this volume's introduction. Kael, we can recall, thought the Maysleses to be unethical in their relations to their pro-filmic subjects because, at least according to Kael, they were said to be unwilling to find a limit to that which they would photograph. In the case of the Beales, it would seem from southernbitch's response, this means that the apparent mental dissolution of the Beales is something we all participate in by simply viewing the film.

While I respect the deep and vivid affective responses that these commentators offer, I would note that there is a longstanding association of female pleasure with pathology and one which we might accidentally reproduce if we judge the Edies' way of living solely as the mark of illness. This problem lies at the heart of the film and is helpful in explaining its enduring pull on viewers. The problem can be summarised as one of the Edies' agency: if we decide to describe and assess the behaviour of each of them as part of a larger matrix of symptoms of mental illness – in short, to diagnose them – then we must also take responsibility for not entirely allowing them to be taken seriously as authors of their lives. When this occurs, we then are prevented from seeing their actions as anything but clues to the delusion that they would seem to suffer from. Conversely, though, if we attribute their behaviours to 'mere eccentricity', do we not also risk losing the sense of the abject and difficult conditions under which they spent the two and a half decades before the Maysleses arrived on their front porch?

The challenge neither to pathologise the Edies nor to dismiss the stringencies of their situation calls for a nuanced response that understands their lives as both eccentrically creative and the results of forces and circumstances often beyond their control. It would seem that the film's hold on its audiences stems from the sense that there is something recognisable about the ways that their lives result from things that they had never anticipated, and yet to which they respond by claiming for themselves some kind of sovereignty, no matter how small. Remembering that, as the previous chapter argued, small gestures within the melodrama are frequently telling of a larger psychological and social experience, we can begin to see how the seemingly inconsequential details of the choice of a scarf or the knotting of a blouse open the way to our seeing the other choices these women insist upon for themselves. In this light, Little Edie's costume is quite revolutionary.

3 'If you can't get a man to propose to you, you might as well be dead!': Direct Cinema and the Problem of Seduction

[Grey Gardens] is oozing with romance, ghosts and other things.

Little Edie Beale

Critics of the melodrama, we should recall, tell us that the figure of the lover who rescues the imperiled heroine from the drudgery of the household typifies the genre, and in a previous chapter I argued that this figure never appears in *Grey Gardens*. In fact, this is only partially true: such a man is indeed within the film, but he is behind the camera rather than in front of it. This is perhaps a first – and singular – instance in documentary film, where a film-maker

becomes, perhaps despite his best wishes, part of a romantic narrative that unfolds before him. And, despite the manner in which the editing of *Grey Gardens* seeks to minimise the impact of this relation between subject and film-maker – specifically, Little Edie and David Maysles – the film is structured by this seductive bond.

While the relation between the Beales and the Maysleses seems to have been in general an affectionate and close one, the sense that another motivation beyond that of the friendly and the familiar takes hold of many viewers as they realise that Little Edie's attention to the Maysleses bears the quality of something between an adolescent crush and an adult infatuation. While many documentary subjects become intimate with the artists who depict them, the fact that Little Edie becomes enamoured with the Maysleses extends well beyond this more general bond between subject and film-maker, and indeed shapes the narrative of *Grey Gardens* in significant ways, not least that the film's story-line becomes that of a failed romance that leaves the two women – and especially the daughter – stranded once again in their household.

This bond between documentary subject and film-maker shapes the manner in which the film depicts its two central figures and has an immensely important effect upon how the Beales perform for the camera and, ultimately, for us, the audience. When we recall that one of the central tenets of direct cinema was to withhold the documentary film-maker's presence in the manufacture of the image and, as much as possible, become as Albert Maysles has frequently said, 'a fly on the wall', we can begin to understand how *Grey Gardens*' makers are more directly implicated in the lives of the Edies than might have been expected. Direct cinema, relying as it does upon a purported agreement among the film-maker, subjects and audience to act as if the presence of the camera does not substantially alter the recorded event, encounters an important problem in *Grey Gardens*: one of the subjects – Little Edie – repeatedly brings the film-makers back into the film by addressing the camera, making eye-contact with the film-makers and discussing her romantic and erotic intensions with the Maysleses and with David specifically. The film's design, then, attempts to address the manner in which the film-makers cannot avoid being implicated in the events and yet seeks to preserve, as much as possible, the direct cinema urge to record events rather than to sponsor them. Of course, claims of non-intervention by any film-maker are suspect, and *Grey Garden*s vividly demonstrates the breakdown of the fictive wall between the Beales and the Maysleses.

The seduction at work is probably less about the specific erotic and romantic attachments to the Maysleses that Little Edie nurtures and more explicitly about her need to have the camera to herself; Little Edie is seducing – in the quite literal sense of the term, where seduction means 'taking down a different path' – the direction that the film will take. More to the point, she is seducing us, her viewers, into believing that her account of the past is valid and trustworthy, particularly over and above that of her mother.

In this regard, *Grey Gardens* as a direct cinema project is always under siege by the Beales. Little Edie, in particular, does not see the camera and microphone as separate from her performance. As the film's narrative unfolds, she discusses her attraction to David and the implications of this for her relation to Albert, to whom she apologises for not finding him as alluring. This dynamic is set into motion from the outset: at an early moment in the film, we see a still, black-and-white photographic image of the Maysleses, Albert holding the camera and David wearing headphones. This image is followed by the first interview with Little Edie and one in which she distinctly appears apart from her mother; Little Edie is overheard greeting the Maysleses for a new day of photography by commenting on their appearances, but only after David Maysles is heard to tell her that she 'looks fantastic'. We hear this important remark before we gain our first glimpse of Little Edie, when she responds to David Maysles' compliment by offering that, 'David, you look absolutely terrific, honestly. Have you got light blue on? Well, Al, you're still … uh [giggles] … Mother says … you're very conservative.' She then flirtatiously changes the subject to the weather and the garden.

This moment is significant in that it offers the first of the Maysleses' images of Little Edie in the film (although we have already seen a still photograph of her in the film's opening montage of newspaper clippings). Important to Little Edie's seduction, this shot emphasises her relation to each of the film-makers and it does so by allowing her gaze – first to David as she offers him a compliment, then to Albert as she sheepishly tries to find something nice to say to him – to define her presence in the film. As we see her through Albert Maysles' lens, she looks directly at them – and views David with a particular affection and desire that is announced the first time that she appears. After this, Little Edie seems never to stop looking. Throughout *Grey Gardens*, her capacity to gaze bestows upon her a sense of presence offered to few women in the more conventional regimes of gendered viewing in the cinema. That is to say, historically women have been denied the possibility to look, and to look with desire – and have subsequently been positioned to be seen, most often by men. Little Edie, by contrast, continuously gazes at the world around her.

I am indebted to Ramzi Fawaz for pointing out that the historical moment in which we discover Little Edie looking in the manner I am describing occurs simultaneously with the emergence of film criticism that discovers how effectively the system of viewing most associated with Hollywood narrative cinema – but in many other kinds of cinema as well – had traditionally relegated women within the cinematic frame to the position of objects. The most famous instance (and one that has shaped the debates about cinema, sexuality and gender) is Laura's Mulvey's 1975 essay, 'Visual Pleasure and Narrative Cinema', in which Mulvey offered that women in the classical Hollywood system were deprived of the gaze – they could quite literally not be seen as having desiring looks of their own, lest they risk punishment within a film's narrative.[23] The fact that feminist critiques of such structured systems of the gaze were appearing at the same moment that the Maysleses were taking the camera and microphone to record a subject like Little Edie – herself trained in the photographic regimes of looking and posing – tells us of an important shift occurring in *Grey Gardens*, one from the figure of the desiring woman who is incapable of being seen as desirous to that of a woman who looks unabashedly and whose gaze organises the film at key moments.

And how very much we witness Little Edie's gaze: at Grey Gardens, at her mother (recall her mother's playful threat that she will 'get naked'), at herself, at her photographs and her portraits, at her beloved books (which she reads with a magnifying glass) and, not least, at the Maysleses. Given the film's tendency to be frequently organised by Little Edie's visual field, the masculinist and heteronormative dimensions of more typical direct cinema projects – and at the heart of the classical Hollywood system – stand at a distance from *Grey Gardens*, which emerges as an anomalous instance in which the film-makers are caught in a remarkable bind about Little Edie's gaze and one that gives the film its energies. Simply put, they cannot ignore Little Edie's recognition of them – as both film-makers and objects of flirtation – and this bestows upon her a different status as a woman. Despite the direct cinema invocation to try to remain outside the action, the Maysleses cannot help but offer us the image of a woman-who-looks because those moments of recognition by her form the basis of the film's revelations about the thwarted romantic and erotic possibilities which the Edies are continually in the process of narrating and re-narrating.

Little Edie's seduction, therefore, begins with our discovery that she emerges in the film as a woman who is capable of possessing her own gaze and, simultaneously, one who is sensitive to the effect that her appearance has upon others. Given the fact that the opening conversation she has with the film-makers is followed by her commentary on her 'revolutionary costume', we sense that Little Edie is comfortable as both subject and object of the look. If, as I have argued, the Maysleses organise the film by interleaving individual interviews with Little Edie with scenes in which mother and daughter interact, then *Grey Gardens* can be understood as deriving its narrative force through the repeated rediscovery of Little Edie's capacity to look, to desire and to appear. As Susan Froemke, one of *Grey Gardens*' editors, comments, 'you would never call it an interview film, but if you look at it carefully, Little Edie is always turning to the camera and doing a monologue'.[24] However, her monologues only appear as such because the editing works to conceal that she is in conversation with the Maysleses.

The film oscillates between the more 'public' scenes in which the entire household appears for the camera to those moments in which Little Edie privately holds forth for the film-makers about the topics of conversation we hear about when the two Edies are in the frame. *Grey Gardens* thus relies upon the Maysleses' capacity to get Little Edie alone, to separate her from her mother, and to prompt her to render her version of the stories that are unfolding over the course of the film. We sense this when, for example, Big Edie prompts her daughter to dance for the camera while the two lounge in their bedroom; Little Edie blushes and shyly refuses to dance while her mother is present – especially as her mother takes centre stage and sings to the Maysleses. Later, when she trusts that her mother is out of earshot and thus unable to witness the bond that is emerging between her and the Maysleses, Little Edie dances privately for them. Tellingly, she performs her dance on the house's first floor, a part of Grey Gardens which Big Edie's limited ability effectively puts out of reach to her.

Lest we think that the particular seduction narrative that organises the film is a coincidence, it should be clear that the *Grey Gardens*' editing does not adhere strictly to the order in which it was photographed – that is, there is not a direct correspondence between the temporal order of the film and the actual sequence in which different conversations were recorded. (The primary clue to this takes the form of Little Edie's clothing: different specific ensembles appear and reappear over the course of the film.) The editing works to produce the seduction narrative as the film's central topic because, at heart, the film asks the audience to consider how it might have emerged that Little Edie failed to consolidate a marriage of her own

when she so clearly has a playful and flirtatious side to her. The arc of the film's plot can be seen as a story in which the film-makers arrive as potential suitors (one of the Maylseses is overheard early in the film describing themselves as the 'gentlemen callers', citing Tennessee Williams' stage narrative about a daughter's failed romance, *The Glass Menagerie*), become increasingly insinuated into the household and ultimately come to pose a threat to the mother by nurturing the daughter's fantasy of escape into the arms of a rescuing man.

None of the intimacy that develops over the course of filming between the Maysleses and Little Edie, though, makes sense unless we consider how the stories she seeks to tell about the men she has known need to be imparted away from her mother; given that, as Froemke comments, the film depicts 'the balance of power' between the two women,[25] Big Edie's impulse to counter-narrate her daughter's versions of these stories is too great a burden for Little Edie and she relies upon her opportunities to speak privately with the Maysleses to offer her version of her love-life. The fact that Little Edie seeks to offer such accounts privately to the Maysleses suggests that she has previously not had the occasion in which to speculate about the meanings of her relations to men beyond the terms of failure upon which her mother insists. That is, she has never been able to understand the romantic and erotic dimensions of her life as positive until this moment. The implication for this new possibility is that her insights about the past begin to spill over into her relation to the film-makers themselves, men who seem intensely interested in hearing about her erotic autobiography.

We can understand how all of this plays out when we consider the topic of Jerry. Gerard 'Jerry' Torre was the Beales' teenage handyman and, aside from the Maysleses, the only other person to appear in the film within the private spaces of the Beales' bedroom. Before meeting the Edies, Torre had run away from his Brooklyn home and found work as a gardener in a neighbouring estate in Easthampton. Quite by accident, he stumbled upon the Beales and into the Maysleses' film. As he recounted later,

I had no idea that anybody actually lived there – there were cobwebs all over the vestibule. But I knock on the door, and, sure enough, Edie comes walking down the stairs in one of her turbans. Frankly, I shit a brick, because I thought she was going to report me for trespassing. Instead, she embraced me, stroked my hair, and said, 'Oh, my God – the Marble Faun has arrived.' I had no idea what she meant, but I was enthralled.[26]

Despite the fact that, in the same account, Torre describes his relation to Little Edie as one of a 'sibling rivalry', his presence in the household was seen as full of romantic and erotic potential – not least by Little Edie.

In one conversation about him between the Edies, we hear how Torre figures differently in their imaginations:

LITTLE EDIE   He might as well leave right now, 'cause he's never gonna get it. So that's it.

BIG EDIE   Get what? Sex with you?

LITTLE EDIE	What he's after!
BIG EDIE	He doesn't want any sex with you.
LITTLE EDIE	That's all they're after!
BIG EDIE	An old person like you?
LITTLE EDIE	That's all they're after! So why don't you tell him right now? You should tell him right now so I'm not bothered by him.

'Getting it', as Little Edie articulates Jerry's desire, is what they're all after, but the turn in the conversation where Little Edie suggests that it should be her mother who should deflate whatever aspirations Torre might have towards her daughter suggests that Little Edie has come to rely upon her mother, at least at the level of fantasy, to ward off potential suitors. (This is complicated by the fact that, as we learn years later, Torre spent some of his free time away from Grey Gardens at well-known gay bars such as The Anvil. But, the matter at hand is the Beales' fantasies about him.)[27] While it may seem unlikely that Torre's presence in the household is motivated, as Little Edie would have it, by his proximity to her, remarkable about this exchange is how her typical narration about her relations to men – extending back to her youth – has her mother thwarting her erotic interests consistently and, thus, once again Big Edie must be relied upon to forestall whatever intentions a man has towards Little Edie. In a remarkable turn of events, Little Edie is not complaining about her mother's ability to shut down a relation to a man, but in fact is insisting that her mother do so. Little Edie's seductions turn, therefore, on a combination of factors that are part of so many romance fantasies, not least the addition of a rival for sexual and romantic attention – here, Jerry – and a combination of avowal and disavowal of motives.

The film's various narrative elements converge in a sequence near the film's end, frequently referred to by the film's directors and its devotees as the 'pink room' scene. This sequence was the very first that was edited from the initial footage made by the Maysleses and, as such, formed the touchstone around which the rest of the film was

subsequently organised.[28] It follows a conversation between Little
Edie and the film-makers about her fear that Jerry might be moving
in with the Beales – an event Little Edie feels is augured by his having
given them a washing machine from a neighbouring house. Little
Edie confesses that she cannot stay much longer in the household,
fearing as she does that her relation with her mother will be disrupted
by Jerry's introduction into their domesticity. But, as we learn in the
pink room sequence, the spectre of men in the household is always a
potentially threatening one, and the conversation that unfolds
between the Edies is the film's culmination of anger, resentment,
sorrow and misgivings about how each woman sees herself as having
arrived in the circumstances in which they live.

The sequence innocently enough captures the Edies as they have
breakfast with the Maysleses in a pink bedroom on the house's
second floor. It opens with Little Edie singing – rather hoarsely and in
an exaggerated fashion – as she lays out the breakfast dishes and as
her mother settles into a chair in the corner. Little Edie waltzes

around the room and ignores her mother; Big Edie then demands that Little Edie stop singing, and when her daughter refuses and leaves the room, Big Edie soliloquises for the Maysleses about how her daughter always needed 'a strong hand' to guide her behaviour. At one point, Big Edie implies that Little Edie prohibited her from allowing Phelan Beale back into the house, and thus suggests that the dissolution of her marriage came about because of her daughter's disavowal of her father. Little Edie then re-enters the room, still singing, and the women continue to bicker as Little Edie addresses her song to David Maysles, at one point crooning 'and I'm in love with YOU!' as she points to David (who is behind the camera) and throws her gaze at him.

Enraged, Big Edie stands up from her chair and haltingly crosses the room, shouting at her daughter that she should stop singing and repeating her threat from an earlier sequence that her bathing suit will come off and reveal her nudity. Little Edie complains that 'I can't have any fun in this house' and then exits to the exterior terrace where we see her sun-bathing and commenting loudly that 'I think mother's very mean to me.' Her mother indirectly responds by commenting to the film-makers that 'she's got a beautiful voice, but you've never heard it'. When Little Edie re-enters the room, her mother makes a conciliatory gesture by asking her to sing 'Only a Rose', and the two of them sing a few lines of the song together.

What subsequently unfolds forms the climax of the narrative and was made to serve as such by the film's editors, Ellen Hovde, Muffie Meyer and Susan Froemke, who remark on the film's DVD-commentary that they screened the footage for this sequence early in the editing process and decided to make it the culmination of the film. The conversation between Big Edie and Little Edie is at moments lyrical and associative and at other moments blunt and graphic in the affective terms it raises, and it is worth quoting at length because, in a film comprised largely of talk, this is talk that both embraces and wounds.

LITTLE EDIE   I don't think there's any point in my meeting anybody that doesn't like music, do you, mother? 'Cause I can't stand them. Finally; I can't stand them. There's something lacking; and it's music; isn't it? I mean; in a man.

BIG EDIE   Well, it is nice to have a man who can play the piano for you.

LITTLE EDIE   No; that isn't all. [To the camera] She doesn't get it.

BIG EDIE   You can practice.

LITTLE EDIE   Unless a man understands music, there's no point in my even meeting him ... 'cause I never could figure out what was wrong. You know; with stockbrokers and tennis players and – I tell you who was a songwriter and a dancer and a playwright and everything, Eugene Tyszkiewicz. [To the camera] But Mother got rid of him in fifteen minutes.

The two women bicker momentarily and then the conversation turns specifically to an opportunity in which Little Edie considers herself to

have had the chance to marry and to leave the household. In the most emotionally raw moment in the film, the Edies prove themselves capable of revealing their personal truths in stark terms:

LITTLE EDIE	And he actually proposed, under the window.
BIG EDIE	He had no home. He was living in a third-class hotel.
LITTLE EDIE	Under the window.
BIG EDIE	He didn't have a thing.
LITTLE EDIE	He said, 'Edith, if you want to get married, I'll marry you.'
BIG EDIE	Not one single nickel.
LITTLE EDIE	And I think that was decent, don't you?
BIG EDIE	I don't see why.
LITTLE EDIE	He probably wouldn't have, but just the same. Not one person had entered Grey

	Gardens for many years … before Eugene Tyszkiewicz came around. So I credit him with all the nerve in the world. [Her voice begins to break.] Why, no one would even speak to us. People who I had walked to the Maidstone Club with for years …
BIG EDIE [to the Maysleses]	Don't believe a word of it.
LITTLE EDIE	Admiring all the other people.
BIG EDIE	Don't believe a word of it, kid. Not a word.
LITTLE EDIE	All the other people …
BIG EDIE [to Little Edie]	If your father could hear you, he'd turn in his grave. He'd say 'My God, Edie!'
LITTLE EDIE	Well; anyway; I think you were very cruel, mother.
BIG EDIE	Well, I don't think it's nice.
LITTLE EDIE [again to the Maysleses]	He came from one of the best families in Poland. And he was related to the Obelenskys. And I think it's terrible that she wouldn't give me a chance with Eugene Tyszkiewicz. I think that was absolutely cruel to drive the only beau away …
BIG EDIE	Do you want to marry a man?
LITTLE EDIE	I don't care! That was the only one, besides these horrible people that came around here.
BIG EDIE [to the film-makers]	Have you got your thing [the camera] lighted for that [i.e., Little Edie]?
DAVID MAYSLES	Yeah; we're all lit.
LITTLE EDIE	He was only thirty-two and from a very good family and she got rid of him in fifteen minutes flat.

BIG EDIE	No, he didn't. He said …
LITTLE EDIE	I'm bored with all these awful people like Jerry and all those people! [Little Edie exits room to exterior terrace.]
BIG EDIE [directly to camera]	That wasn't the truth. No. Tell him the truth. That was not the truth. Uh, no, and that was not the truth. He said, 'How could such a warm, lovely person over the telephone turn into anything so cold?' That's what he said right down on the porch. So I said, I said, 'You'd better go home.' Never said goodbye or anything. 'How could such a warm, lovely woman over the telephone turn into something so cold?' I thought that was just a little too much.

Remarkable about this sequence is that the Edies narrate a failed marriage proposal by commenting on the specific places in the house where events in the story are remembered to have occurred: Little Edie recalls Tyszkiewicz as proposing beneath one of the house's windows, while her mother responds by recounting how she had to send her daughter's suitor away while on the house's porch. The house's built space, its rooms, porches and windows, has become entwined with the past, an association that happens repeatedly within the film – earlier, after giving a tour of the house, Little Edie has told the film-makers that 'It's very difficult to keep the line between the past and the present. Do you know what I mean? It's awfully difficult.'

What do we make, then, of the fact that Albert Maysles has commented that when he contacted Eugene Tyszkiewicz in order to secure a release to use his name in the film, Tyszkiewicz told Maysles that he had only been to Grey Gardens once, and that was to enquire about whether the property was for sale. While it is hard to know the circumstances under which the Beales' competing versions of this romance came about, if we entertain the possibility that random visitors to the house might so easily become the topic of such rampant dispute, then we can begin to get a sense that virtually every topic that they might take up centres, in the end, on Little Edie's yearned-for return to New York and Big Edie's insistence that her daughter did not have the capacity to maintain the social life which she wanted to resume. Grey Gardens is a haunted house for the Beales because it is quite literally where their fantasies about themselves reside – fantasies which can, of course, be true enough for the person who experiences them.

Yet, in a strange coincidence of their accounts, each recognises that the mother's terms are the ones that must be honoured, and in this regard Little Edie's anger at her mother's perceived prohibition from leaving the household is conjoined with her deeply formed need to have Big Edie's approval. When Little Edie comments that 'this is my mother's house', she reveals more than she perhaps even intends, because if the house is a psychic space as much as it is a physical one – that is, it hosts memories, fantasies and emotions – then her mother owns the terms through which those things will be negotiated.

Lest we think that this conversation forms some kind of reckoning for the two Edies, one in which the terms of their bonds might change or be redefined, it seems more likely to be the case that this outburst repeats the terms of their shared domestic life that have been in place since perhaps the early 1950s. It seems that they could well have been fighting over any topic – Jerry, Eugene Tyszkiewicz, their rejection by the members of the Maidstone Club – for twenty years, if not longer. Thus, when Little Edie poignantly reconciles herself to the fact that 'this is my mother's house', she looks at the late summer seascape and the trees newly bare of their leaves and sighs, 'Oh, God … another winter.' Another winter of the conversations we have just witnessed for nearly ninety minutes and which bind mother and daughter together.

But, as usual, Little Edie's comments in the same closing sequence disclose an intelligence and wit that buoys her in such painful moments, and in her final remarks to the Maysleses, with the water and the garden in early autumn light, her thoughts are poetic, funny, melancholic and, strangely, still tinged with hope. The sequence combines two sequences photographed at different moments. In the first, she calmly professes:

So, you just can't do anything about it. So I can see now why girls get married. You know, they're forced into it. It's all a question of who you want to stay with. Of course, I'm mad about animals, but raccoons and cats become a little bit boring. I mean, for too long a time. I don't know. I don't know. I better check on Mother and the cats. She's a lot of fun. I hope she doesn't die. I hate to spend the winter here; though. Oh, God. Another winter.

After a shot panning the façade of Grey Gardens and the sound of the chilly wind in the trees, we discover Little Edie dressed for autumn in long coat of black leather, her face without makeup and in stark close-up. Her voice trembles and she seems frail and afraid as she whispers her final spoken words of the film:

Very depressing, you know, when winter sets in here. You know, 'cause I don't like the country, and I don't want to be here. Any little rat – any little rat's nest in New York, any little mouse hole … [her voice quakes with repressed tears] … any little rat hole, even on Tenth Avenue, I would like better.

With that, she turns and, slamming the house's door behind her, disappears into Grey Garden's falling-down gloom.

A sound-bridge and shots of raccoons pulling at the food left for them ushers us to *Grey Gardens*' coda. The film closes with images of Big Edie drowsily reciting the words to Cole Porter's 'Night and Day' while lying amid the squalor of the cat-strewn bedroom. Hovde, Meyer and Froemke's editing leaves mother and daughter joined by the soundtrack: we hear Big Edie murmuring, 'No matter, darling where you are/I think of you/Night and day/In the silence of my lonely room/I think of you', and she curls upon her bed in near sleep. Downstairs, Little Edie dances by herself in a self-enclosed reverie, framed by the grand and decrepit staircase's banisters; dressed now in a form-fitting ensemble of black lace and turning elegantly in her white high-heels, she hums 'The magic of dreams come true'. The camera pivots to darkness.

If Little Edie had hoped to seduce the film-makers, she only half-succeeded. In the film's final shot, she seems to make eye-contact with the camera through the banisters and to acknowledge that she is the film's compelling visual presence and the subject about which her mother, in Porter's terms, thinks of in the silence of her lonely room. But, if Little Edie has captured the Maysleses, Hovde, Meyer, Froemke and us, she then pivots away and returns to the private hermetic world of her dreams, and this final gesture tells us as much about what we can claim to know of the Beales as anyone. They are

by turns enchanting and compelling but also distant and ultimately unknowable.

If the relation between mother and child forms the nexus through which so many claims of identity can be made, then the raw materials of that relation do become, as much as they might, known in *Grey Gardens*. Uncomfortable forms of intimacy, loss, aging, the prospect of death, but also joy, humour, pleasure, wit and self-knowledge become possible for the Edies and indeed seem inevitable. Albert Maysles remarks that the life we see on camera hardly differs from what the Beales lived well before he and his brother arrived at the Beales' home; he tells us on the DVD director's commentary that he and his brother would often hear the Beales through the house's open windows as they approached to start a day's filming and that the women would still be talking as the two men left. Perhaps they did not need the melodrama's rescuing hero to pull them from the house – indeed, perhaps they never meant to leave in the first place.

Conclusion: 'I'm pulverized by this latest thing': *Grey Gardens* and its Lives

One measure of *Grey Gardens*' appeal to its audiences has been the comparatively large number of texts – films, stage performances, fashion imagery, blogs, fan commentary – that have responded to and extended the meanings of the Maysleses' original film. It is difficult to imagine how a film of its sort – with its meagre budget, small cast and seemingly limited appeal – might take hold of its viewers and summon from them so many different kinds of cultural productions. Further, these texts seem hardly to be derivative; that is, they do not seem cynically to be seeking to exploit the success of the film as much as they express the needs of the film's audiences to offer their interpretations of the meanings of *Grey Gardens*. As previously discussed, *Grey Gardens* seems to demand much from its viewers to offer their explanations of what the film means to them. *Grey Gardens* in this regard is both a film and an idea, and from the texts sponsored by the Maysleses' film we learn that its viewers are eager to extend the idea to their own lives.

In the brief space of this conclusion, it would be impossible to consider in detail each of *Grey Gardens*' successors, and here I would offer two that are worth examining for starkly divergent reasons. *The Beales of Grey Gardens*, the 2006 release from Maysles films, is the most explicit supplement to the first film, comprised as it is of footage of the Beales from the Maysleses' own film archives. In contrast, *Grey Gardens*, a 2009 feature film that showcased the talents of actresses Jessica Lange and Drew Barrymore, restages portions of the 1975 film while simultaneously interspersing scenes set in earlier moments in the Beales' lives from the 1930s to the 1970s. The former augments its forebear with images and sounds that expand our sense of how the Beales lived their everyday lives, while the latter invokes the name of the original film in order to offer a Hollywood-style rendering of how Big Edie and Little Edie lost their wealth and the affective dimensions of this loss. One is supplemental fact while the other is fantasised fiction.

It is no exaggeration to say that *The Beales of Grey Gardens* supplements *Grey Gardens* in that the later film makes little sense without having seen the first of the Maysleses' films about the Beales. The supplement that *The Beales of Grey Gardens* offers to the original film was initiated, we learn, from Albert Maysles' sense that the original film's compelling version of events omitted much of the play between the Edies and the Maysleses. (David Maysles died in January 1987 while he and his brother were at work on various film projects about the contemporary artist Christo, the building of the J. Paul Getty Museum in Los Angeles and new treatments for heart disease.) Albert Maysles suggests that *Grey Gardens* was, by design, meant to emphasise the relation between Big Edie and Little Edie, but that the raw footage that was not included in the first film's final version could offer a more robust sense of the conditions under which the film was made – not least the importance of the Maysleses themselves within the film's *mise en scène*.

If we consider *The Beales of Grey Gardens* to function as an interpretation of the first film – one, of course, with the advantage of being offered by someone who was present at the first film's making – then how does it augment or alter our sense of *Grey Gardens*? Largely, it does not change our more general impressions of the Edies – they remain the eccentric, vivacious and neurotic figures that emerge in the 1975 release – and the materials included in the subsequent film affirm the tendencies at work in the first film and which are discussed in this book. Two such aspects are worth identifying specifically, though: the first is the sense of how these women were highly anomalous figures because of the manner in which their pleasures in looking were recorded throughout the making of the film; and the second is the fantastic sartorial excesses which were a part of their daily lives. These two aspects conjoin themselves in the way that they confirm the flirtatious and seductive relation between Little Edie and David Maysles.

Worth emphasising in *The Beales of Grey Gardens*, then, are several key sequences that reveal the Edies to have been playfully engaged with the Maysleses in the photographic process. In one startling moment, for example, we discover Big Edie lying on her back on the floor of their outdoor terrace as she holds a camera to her eye and takes still pictures of the film-makers. We hear the conversation between the Maysleses and Big Edie as they coach her to frame the images she is making of them. Their camera and microphone continue to record her as she records them, and she proves herself to be an astute student who took instruction well – the proof of such are the still images which we then see reproduced within the film. The elegantly composed black-and-white images of the brothers, relaxed and smiling as they look at Big Edie, confirm the presence of people who are enjoying themselves in the company of valued friends. More importantly, this moment serves to reverse our assumptions of how this woman saw herself because the first film (i.e., *Grey Gardens*) presents her as immobile and frequently indifferent to the image she presents of herself, while this sequence in the later film suggests that she was more capable of going where she pleased – with help, it would seem – and that she was curious about the process of photography that was being undertaken in her house. It would thus seem to be perhaps only a slight overstatement to say that the prospect of a woman engaged in the making of an image of those who made images of her is an uncommon turnabout in the visual regime of gender.

The virtuosity of Little Edie's fashions emerges in the film with greater force than in the first release and is discovered to have been a joint effort between mother and daughter. One sequence, titled 'Fashion', consists of a montage of Little Edie's carefully composed ensembles – the upside-down skirts, the blouses fastened with safety pins, the always-present head-scarf – set to the non-diegetic musical accompaniment of Hildegarde's version of Dorothy Fields and

Jerome Kern's ballad, 'I dream too much'. Prior to this montage, though, the Maysleses include a conversation about fashion that suggests how much Little Edie's physical presence was shaped by her mother. Inevitably, they argue:

BIG EDIE [to her daughter]	Could you put on that black thing that I love so much.
LITTLE EDIE	Oh, Mother, that's a nightgown. I wouldn't think of it.
BIG EDIE	Why not? They wear those things – they look like evening dresses.
DAVID MAYSLES [to Big Edie]	How many times does Edie have to change costumes to make you happy?
BIG EDIE	Oh, about ten [times a day].

They then continue to bicker about whether the dress under discussion is a nightgown or an evening dress; Big Edie finally interjects while looking at the Maysleses, 'Don't get them excited. Put the damn thing on!'

This is the only moment in either of the films in which we see the Beales self-consciously discussing how to present themselves for the Maysleses, and the film-makers use the occasion to ask them in more pointed fashion about the pleasures that Little Edie's costumes give to her mother. The fact that, as Big Edie blithely comments, she prompts her daughter to change her clothing ten times a day helps to understand how Little Edie's remarkable ensembles were not solely of her invention, and that it seems to have been a chore for her to please her mother by dressing for her. Thus, Big Edie's remark to her daughter that she not 'get them [i.e., the Maysleses] excited' shifts Little Edie's seductive behaviour and appearance from that of pleasing herself to a larger dynamic in which her mother participates. More pointedly, Little Edie's fashions form a bond between mother and daughter that serves to infantilise the daughter, rendering her as a child both seeking her mother's approval in her choice of clothing and resenting the maternal control over when and how she should appear. In this regard, Little Edie's complaints that she felt trapped in her mother's house become all the more poignant.

If *The Beales of Grey Gardens* expands our sense of the bond between the Beales and the relation they had to Albert and David Maysles, *Grey Gardens*, the 2009 feature film, produced for distribution on the Home Box Office cable channel, re-narrates the Beales story by making explicit what can only remain tacit in the non-fiction films: it recuperates the past for *Grey Gardens*' audiences by depicting events that remain largely the Beales' fantasies of the past. That is, the past depicted by the HBO film *Grey Gardens* relies upon versions of the events that the Edies discuss in the Maysleses' films, but these events cannot be corroborated to have occurred in the manner that the HBO film tells us. This is not to argue that the fiction film somehow gets the events wrong, but to ask about the particular story it tells about the Beales, and which it wants to suggest tells us about the meaning of their lives.

Two events within the HBO version, for example, organise the Beales story in telling ways: the departure of Big Edie's friend and musical accompanist, George 'Gould' Strong, and Little Edie's return to Grey Gardens from New York in the early 1950s. The film depicts the earlier event as the result of a thwarted erotic bond between Big Edie and Gould in that Gould seems to stay at Grey Gardens largely to take advantage of the Beales' wealth. In order to do such, we see him avoiding Big Edie's romantic and sexual advances – with strong implications that his lack of interest in her stems from a more general lack of interest in women (taking advantage of the longer-standing stereotype of the musically inclined queer man). As the Beales' wealth dwindles, Big Edie emerges as a recognisable type within the popular culture's imagination of female sexuality: the desperate woman. In this characterisation, a woman whose lover departs usually is clinging and needful – even if, as seems the case offered by the HBO version, her lover never was her lover to begin with.

The second event – Little Edie's return to Grey Gardens in the early 1950s – is thus conjoined with Gould's departure and serves to vilify the mother by suggesting that she curtailed her daughter's life and professional career in Manhattan in order to install her daughter in the place where her (failed) romance once was. Thus we see Little Edie returning to a dishevelled house strewn with litter and in need of a servant to maintain it – she walks through the house's front door and casts sideward glances tinged with sorrow and disgust at the prospect of having to live with her mother.

The HBO version thus narrates the inaugural events of their newly impoverished life not as the result of the control that men exerted over their financial lives – the reader will remember Big Edie's telegram to her brother which opens this book – but as the mother's failure to 'keep a man in her life' because of her eccentricity. In this regard, the 2009 version seems much more conservative in its understanding of these women than the Maysleses' original film because the non-fiction version could maintain an ambiguity about the women's motives and wishes in a way that the fictionalised account refuses to.

As usual, though, the actual events of the Beales' lives serve to defy belief in a way that no fictional account ever could. When Edith Ewing Bouvier Beale died on 5 February 1977 at the local hospital after a fall in her home, she was buried in the Catholic Cemetery in Easthampton and, after her death, Little Edie realised her fantasy of public performance by giving eight shows in January 1978 at the Reno Sweeney cabaret in Manhattan, a short-lived career that earned her a cult-like following among her devotees but also garnered a blistering review in *The New York Times* that described her act as 'a public display of ineptitude'.[29]

She also continued to live for two years in the house that had been her mother's and sold the property in 1979, stipulating that the buyers could not tear down the house. After the sale of Grey Gardens, Little Edie lived in New York City, Montreal and California, but spent the last years of her life living in a modest apartment in Bal Harbour, Florida, and corresponding with her family and some of her fans from the film. She died of a heart attack in 2002 at the age of eighty-four and was cremated and interred near the remains of her brother, Bouvier 'Buddy' Beale, at a cemetery in Long Island – but not next to her mother.

The financial situation for the Beales did not seem to have been altered by the making of *Grey Gardens*, each woman having negotiated with the Mayslesses for a fee of $5,000 for participating in the film – hardly a sum to make much difference in their lives. After the film's release, Little Edie complained in her correspondence to friends that she thought the film-makers should have paid them more and suggested that there were residual payments due to them that the film-makers should have honoured; however, there is no documentation to confirm such was ever negotiated. Indeed, Little Edie hinted to friends that, when she decided to sell Grey Gardens, she deliberately sold the house for less than it was worth in order to spite her family, who she thought would want the property. Thus, her need for financial support was, as always and in the terms that she shared with her mother, cross-hatched with her desire to remain her own woman.

The house itself has been renovated by the purchasers, Benjamin Bradlee, who was executive editor of *The Washington Post* during the Watergate scandal, and his wife, the journalist Sally Quinn. In a 2005 film about the life of the house and its famous former owners, *Ghosts of Grey Gardens*, film-maker Liliana Greenfield-Sanders revisits Grey Gardens and photographs its restored elegance, while Quinn recounts that Little Edie insisted that her mother's furnishings – those few that remained – stay with the house. She also tells us that Lois Wright – the family friend who briefly appears in the film at Big Edie's birthday party – told her that she had heard from Big Edie from beyond the grave and that Big Edie was pleased with the sale.

Thus, Grey Gardens has returned to its status as a summer retreat for the wealthy and privileged, while *Grey Gardens* remains the fragile record of the house's earlier paradoxical decline into physical decrepitude and symbolic ascent into the poetics of cinema. The experience of seeing the rooms in Greenfield-Sanders' film as Quinn and Bradlee now live in them – rebuilt, freshly painted, full of antiques and art – is unexpectedly poignant, revealing that the squalor in which the Beales lived expressed a powerful artistic temperament and yet a shared life full of loss, sadness and deprivation.

An important lesson of *Grey Gardens* is that it is too easy to render Big Edie and Little Edie as heroines of a resistant femininity – what Little Edie would call being 'staunch' – because such a fantasy requires us to neglect the steep costs demanded by these women's remarkable independence. Put another way, it is one thing to want the Beales' eccentricities for them, but more challenging to consider making the apparently necessary sacrifices ourselves. And, it would be a mistake to consider them forerunners of feminist independence, not least because their manner of living was sponsored by their sense of themselves as patricians in the American class system as much as it was by any need to express themselves – that is, they did not seem to see their lives as characterised by loss of wealth as much as a loss of the creative opportunities that they thought themselves entitled to pursue.

Albert Maysles tells us in *The Beales of Grey Gardens* that when Big Edie was dying, her daughter asked her if there were anything else she wanted to say and that her response was that it was 'all in the film'. No life, of course, can ever entirely be contained within a single text, but a glimpse of an idea about one's life – what it was, what one wants it to be – can, under the best of circumstances, be captured. The continuing appeal of Edith Ewing Beale and Edith Bouvier Beale for audiences of the many texts that now claim the name of Grey Gardens tells us of an important shift in the politics of everyday life, a shift that is made possible by the realisation that the Beales did not appear in the film simply as impoverished and pathetic losers. That, I would argue, would have been their status were the film made ten years earlier than it was. Appearing when it did, though – on the heels of mainstream feminism, the countercultures of the 1960s that were taking hold within the popular imagination more widely and in the context of a non-Hollywood metropolitan cinema – their impoverishment became a badge of honour (not least in Little Edie's fashions, for example) and their pathos was revealed to have been not something that their audiences felt *for* them, but something that they shared *with* the larger world. Their willingness to experiment with their lives and to find the language – the dazzling, crazy, fun, haunting language – that they gave and that they still give to us makes them more compelling than ever and makes us, even just a little bit, wish that we could return to Grey Gardens, sit on Big Edie's bed and have Little Edie play records for us.

Notes

1 Bill Nichols, *Representing Reality: Issues and Concepts in Documentary* (Bloomington: Indiana University Press, 1991), p. 44.

2 Paul Ward, *Documentary: The Margins of Reality* (London: Wallflower Press, 2005), p. 14.

3 Michael Renov, *The Subject of Documentary* (Minneapolis: University of Minnesota Press, 2004), p. 174.

4 Renov, *The Subject of Documentary*, p. 181.

5 Pauline Kael, 'Gimme Shelter', *The New Yorker Magazine*, 19 December 1970, p. 112.

6 Marcia Landy, *Imitations of Life: A Reader* (Detroit: Wayne State University Press, 1991), p. 14.

7 Kristine McKenna, *Talk to Her: Interviews* (Seattle: Fantagraphics, 2004), p. 14.

8 Peter Brooks, 'The Melodramatic Imagination', in Landy, *Imitations of Life*, p. 56.

9 McKenna, *Talk to Her*, p. 14.

10 John David Rhodes, '"Concentrated Ground": *Grey Gardens* and the Cinema of the Domestic', *Framework* vol. 47 no. 1, Spring 2006, p. 92.

11 Sigmund Freud, 'Family Romances', in *The Freud Reader*, ed. Peter Gay (New York: Norton, 1989), p. 299.

12 Freud, 'Family Romances', p. 300.

13 Eva Marie Beale, *Edith Bouvier Beale of Grey Gardens: A Life in Pictures*, ed. Anne Verlhac (Paris: Verlhac Editions, 2009).

14 Beale, *Edith Bouvier Beale of Grey Gardens*, pp. 182–3.

15 Andy Warhol, *The Philosophy of Andy Warhol* (New York: Harvest Books, 1975), p. 65.

16 Ibid., p. 54.

17 Pamela Church Gibson, '"No One Expects Me Anywhere": Invisible Women, Ageing and the Fashion Industry', in Stella Bruzzi and Pamela Church Gibson (eds), *Fashion Cultures: Theories, Explorations and Analysis* (London: Routledge, 2001), p. 81.

18 <jezebel.com/5082342/little-edie-beale-the-ultimate-recessionista>, accessed 14 March, 2010.

19 Ibid.

20 Ibid.

21 ibid.

22 Ibid.

23 Laura Mulvey, 'Visual Pleasure and Narrative Cinema', *Screen* vol. 16 no. 3, pp. 6–18.

24 Liz Stubbs, *Documentary Filmmakers Speak* (New York: Allworth Press, 2002), p. 27.

25 Sheila Curran Bernhard, *Documentary Storytelling for Video and Filmmakers* (Burlington, MA: Focal Press, 2004), p. 230.

26 Adam Green, 'The Marble Faun', *The New Yorker*, 6 March 2006, p. 13.

27 Ibid.

28 *Grey Gardens* DVD commentary.

29 *The New York Times*, 12 January 1978.

Credits

Grey Gardens
USA 1975

Directed by
David Maysles
Albert Maysles
Ellen Hovde
Muffie Meyer
Producers
The Maysles brothers
A Portrait Films, Inc.,
Production
Associate Producer
Susan Froemke
Filmed by
Albert Maysles
David Maysles
Edited by
Ellen Hovde
Muffie Meyer
Susan Froemke

© 1975 Portrait Films,
Inc.
Production Company
Portrait Films, Inc.,
presents a Maysles
Brothers' Film

Sound Mixer
Lee Dichter
Sound Mixing
Photo-Mag
Color Negative
EFX Unlimited Inc.
Negative Timing
Morris Schlein
Precision/Deluxe

Thanks to the following
individuals and
organisations for their
help:
Marianne Barcellona
Peter Beard
Harry Benson
Alan Bomser
Charlie – Projectionist,
Movielab
Cynthia Castleman
Pamela Degnan
Kathryn Demby
Holly Gill
Bernard Gotfryd
John Jourdan
Dorothy King
Donald Klocek
Akiva Kohane
Sarah Legon
Vincent Lombardo
Noelle Penraat
Vincent Stenerson
TVC Laboratories
Trans/Audio
Lois Wright

The Robert Frost Estate
for permission to include
lines from 'The Road Not
Taken' as spoken. The
correct lines are:

Two roads diverged in a
yellow wood,
And sorry I could not
travel both …
…………………………
…………………………
I took the one less
travelled by,
And that has made all
the difference.

From 'The Road Not
Taken' from *The Poetry of
Robert Frost*, edited by
Edward Connery Lathem.
Copyright 1916, © 1969
by Holt, Rinehart and
Winston. Copyright 1944
by Robert Frost. Used by
permission of Holt,
Rinehart and Winston,
Publishers.

CAST
Edith Bouvier Beale
Herself
Edith 'Little Edie'
Bouvier Beale
Herself
Brooks Hiers
Himself (gardener)
Norman Vincent Peale
Himself (voice)

Uncredited
Jack Helmuth (Birthday Guest)
Himself
Albert Maysles
Himself
David Maysles
Himself
Jerry Torre (handyman)
Himself
Lois Wright (birthday guest)
Herself

Production Details
Filmed in 1973 on location at Grey Gardens, Easthampton, Long Island, New York, USA. 35mm; EFX Color; 1.37:1. US theatrical release by Portrait Films, Inc., on 19 February 1976 (New York Film Festival premiere on 27 September 1975). Running time: 95 minutes/8,534 feet

405220

Don't miss out! Sign up to receive news about BFI Film and TV Classics and win a free bundle of books worth £100!

Each book in the BFI Film and TV Classics series honours a landmark of world cinema and television.

With new titles publishing every year, the series represent some of the best writing on film and TV available in print today.

discover film

In order to enter, first sign up via: http://www.palgrave.com/resources/mailing.asp and then simply email bfi@palgrave.com with your name, email address and NEW BFI CONTACT in the subject header.

Entry offer ends: 04/01/12. The winner will be contacted via email by 31/01/12.